Paine,
Scripture,
and Authority

James Gillray. "Fashion before Ease;—Or, A Good Constitution Sacrificed, for a Fantastick Form." 2 January 1793.

[Gillray's anti-Republican caricature presents a drunk Tom Paine with a tape inscribed *Rights of Man* hanging from his pocket. He places his foot on the posterior of a defenseless and "pained" Britannia in a French stay as she clings to an oak tree for stability.]

Paine,
Scripture,
and Authority

The Age of Reason
as Religious
and Political Idea

Edward H. Davidson
and William J. Scheick

Bethlehem: Lehigh University Press
London and Toronto: Associated University Presses

Associated University Presses
440 Forsgate Drive
Cranbury, NJ 08512

Associated University Presses
25 Sicilian Avenue
London WC1A 2QH, England

Associated University Presses
P.O. Box 338, Port Credit
Mississauga, Ontario
Canada L5G 4L8

The paper used in this publication meets the requirements of the American National Standard for Permanence of Paper for Printed Library Materials Z39.48-1984.

Library of Congress Cataloging-in-Publication Data

Davidson, Edward H. (Edward Hutchins)
Paine, Scripture, and authority : the Age of reason as religious and political idea / Edward H. Davidson and William J. Scheick
p. cm.
Includes bibliographical references and index
ISBN 0-934223-29-7 (alk. paper)
1. Paine, Thomas, 1737–1809. Age of reason. 2. Rationalism. 3. Bible—Inspiration—History of doctrines—18th century. 4. Bible—Evidences, authority, etc.—History of doctrines—18th century. 5. Authority (Religion)—History of doctrines—18th century. 6. Christianity and politics—History of doctrines—18th century. 7. Radicalism—History—18th century. 8. Enlightenment. I. Scheick, William J. II. Paine, Thomas, 1737–1809. Age of reason. III. Title.
BL2740.D38 1994
211'.5—dc20 92-55135
CIP

PRINTED IN THE UNITED STATES OF AMERICA

For Ann
and
For Catherine

Contents

Preface

For many years Paine's *Age of Reason* has fascinated and disturbed me. I first came upon it during my youth when I was a believer in the literal truth of the Bible and when I accepted the teachings of the church in which I had been reared. At that impressionable time of my youth I was not so much shaken by Paine's argument as I was made aware of something different from what I believed. I found that I could entertain another set of ideas about religion from those in which I had been instructed. I thought it then, and I think it still, an interesting and tantalizing book, more problematic than its sharply satirical, commonsensical manner makes it appear.

It was largely my memory of that first difficulty I experienced in my youth and my inability to come to terms with it that persuaded me to undertake a modest enterprise in treating Paine's book as I have come to understand it long after that first impression has become only a memory. I wanted to work out the background to and the logic of that book, and to try to understand it in itself and in relation to the alternative mode of political liberalism that has been concealed beneath its announced and sustained purpose.

—E. H. D.

I first read *The Age of Reason*, or at least substantial parts of it, when I was fifteen. I had received a dogmatic religious training throughout my childhood, and I had developed feelings and thoughts against the grain of that education. My questions were rebuffed rather than answered, and it was no surprise that my curiosity was piqued by a magazine advertisement proffering an inexpensive copy of *The Age of Reason* for open-minded readers. Paine's book arrived in a plain brown envelope, as the advertisement had promised, and I furtively read it, or large parts of it, as a bad, even dangerous, book.

9

That copy of Paine's work is now lost, nor can I recover much of my initial response to it. Whatever of Paine's claims I may or may not have appreciated, I did register his outrage against established religions and his call for a personal emancipation from theological dogma. Paine's seemingly authoritative voice, countering the authorities of dogma, appealed to me at that time.

My return to *The Age of Reason* thirty-five years later seems prompted by the question of Paine's authority as well as by the not-to-be-missed opportunity to collaborate with my coauthor. But perhaps this scholarly trek may instance once more how we retrack old trails more often than we know or for more reasons than we understand—how (contrary to Paine's belief) it is difficult after all for us to break at will with the past.

—W. J. S.

Acknowledgments

Throughout the course of this inquiry we have incurred certain debts. We have depended on the Paine biographers, from the earliest written in Paine's lifetime to the latest. In their own ways, each of them has kept Paine's name before a conscientious and intelligent public opinion. We have had the help of the librarians at the University of Illinois at Champaign-Urbana and the University of Texas at Austin, and the correspondence of friends and colleagues. Our most extensive debts are suggested in the notes to the text, to those who have inquired into and written cogent statements about Paine and his age's ways that require our expression of gratitude. Part of our first chapter appeared as "Authority in Paine's *Common Sense* and *Crisis* Papers," *Studies in the Humanities* 18 (1991): 124–34; and we are grateful to the editors. We acknowledge, as well, the generous assistance of Catherine Rainwater.

Textual Note

All citations to Paine's works refer to the two volumes of *The Complete Writings of Thomas Paine,* edited by Philip S. Foner (New York: Citadel Press, 1945). Page references for quotations from this edition are cited parenthetically in the text with the proper volume number.

Paine,
Scripture,
and Authority

Introduction: "Wounds of Deadly Hate Have Pierced So Deep"

Reviewing the foreground and preparation for Thomas Paine's *Age of Reason* recalls not only what the book was and came to be, specifically in religious discussions, but also what role it played more generally in intellectual history. The 1790s were a time of vital debate over all matters of religious, political, and social thought. Those years were, it hardly needs saying, a time of upheaval; they followed the American Revolution and demarcated the French Revolution. During the 1790s, numerous exponents of certain radical doctrines were heard and read by a wide and varied audience. Various members of this audience worried about the possible effect of this fomentation of radical thought on allegedly simple and ignorant natures presumably susceptible to the insidious contentions of "reformers" such as deists, infidels, and atheists; for these reformers seemed to express notions threatening to the order of society and to the preservation of a way of life precious to their adversaries. *The Age of Reason,* it needs saying at the outset, aimed directly at and came hard upon congeries of principles affecting the thought and action of all manner of people in Western Europe and, as well, in America.

The Age of Reason was, by any measure taken in its time, an irreverent book on the subject of religion, and so it actually is. It gained its place in religious discussion, however, not simply because it stormed the Bible and the Christian church, but also because it came from the arch-radical propagandist, Tom Paine, whose name was sometimes insultingly spelled "Pain" by his ideological opponents. Paine's eventual fame as the defender of the American Revolution was predicated on his notoriety, for some at least, in assuming at the time of the opening of the French Revolution the role of an outspoken radical advocate of civil rebellion.[1] The transition between these two identities occurred during Paine's association with Edmund Burke, which commenced in 1788 and ended in 1791, when *Rights of Man* thrust Paine to the forefront of political radicalism during the last decade of the eighteenth century.

It is altogether likely that without Burke, Paine would hardly have been noticed. Without *Reflections on the Revolution in France,* Burke's defense of the British social order, there would have been no *Rights of Man,* Paine's ideological and personal response to Burke that earned the American patriot extensive international attention. "The great controversy in which Burke and Paine were the principal antagonists," one commentator has declared, "was perhaps the most crucial ideological debate ever carried on in English."[2] Indeed, the Burke-Paine controversy, as centered in the phrase "the Rights of Man," has remained an issue of consequence for two hundred years. For Paine, however, it was also a very personal debate, focused on the nature of authority, and it extended beyond the French Revolution to include religion, the Christian church, and even the Bible.

Curiously, this stage of the controversy concerning human rights—the freedom of people to think and the ways they come to believe and to worship—has received much less attention in the twentieth century than has the Burke-Paine debate. If there has been a virtual library of commentary of the highest order on the issues raised in *Rights of Man,*[3] the contexts and concerns of *The Age of Reason* have been of little interest to scholars today.[4] Paine's renown for *Common Sense,* the *Crisis* papers, and *Rights of Man* has not been sufficient to make *The Age of Reason* attract current critical attention. There was no Burke to highlight it, and Bishop Richard Watson's opposition to it is for us now a forgotten moment of little interest.

Nevertheless, *The Age of Reason* was a sequel to Paine's famous previous writings, especially *Rights of Man.* For all of his religious pretensions, if serious religious argument in *The Age of Reason*, Paine intended the work to provide one more testament to human freedom and political justice. The Bible and the Christian churches—all religions, finally—were for Paine great agents of superstition, political oppression, and civil injustice. Paine maintained that church and state had continually conspired to deprive people of their inherent rights. He spoke for, he prophesied, an age of intellectual freedom, when reason would triumph over superstition, when the natural liberties of humanity would supplant priestcraft and kingship, which were both secondary effects of politically managed foolish legends and religious superstitions. *The Age of Reason* was, in short, a political treatise with a strong religious design. This religious design was constructed with an eye to subverting the political system dependent on religion, with an eye to liberating humanity from ages of oppressive control by the despotic triumvirate of scripture, church, and state.

Paine was, by his own statement, not an atheist. At the outset of *The Age of Reason* he declared that he believed in the one God. What he believed or what he affirmed made little difference, however. In the minds of many of his contemporaries, his book testified to his alliance with nonbelievers, enemies of religion, dangerous persons to the church and to the state. So Thomas Paine was succinctly and reproachfully dubbed Tom Pain.

The contemporary response to *The Age of Reason* emphasized three issues and implied a fourth. One concerned Paine's assault on Scripture as a sacred, canonical text unified by a single design. Paine claimed that the Bible was not an intricate and unbroken unit from beginning to end, but was variously originated, historically dismembered, and narratively fractured. The second issue concerned Paine's claim that Christianity was a man-made religion on the same level of human invention as such Oriental religions as Islam and Hinduism. The third issue concerned Paine's ability propagandistically to manipulate his audience. Paine knew he had one, and so did his detractors. That audience was there immediately because of Paine's reputation as the advocate of the American Revolution; but it was also there because of the times, which had so readied that audience, as it had Paine and his opposition, that answers and objections to stated ideas and beliefs could be anticipated even before they were offered. The fourth issue implied in the response to Paine concerned his manner. Besides expressing himself in a colloquial and abusive style inappropriate to the sacred subject of Scripture, Paine employed the devices common to cheap pamphleteering, political debate, and some novels: scurrility, satire, quotation for insulting effect, and personal and dramatic asides. All four considerations figured in the incensed hostility and responses aroused by *The Age of Reason,* a reaction matched by few other books in its time.

All four of these concerns may have been, to some extent, pertinent to the times and to the book Paine wrote, but finally they did not directly close with what he intended to do. Although several of his contemporaries worried, even became frantic in some instances, about the possible social effects of *The Age of Reason,* they had only a vague impression of the *political* dimension of the book. They sensed *generally* that it was a politically dangerous writing, and after Paine's death his commentary on Scripture would even be banned from publication in England. However, these early glimmerings of political consequence notwithstanding, readers for nearly two hundred years have failed to assess fully the political objective, the original reason, behind the religious argument and design of Paine's book.

One main purpose of this study is, therefore, to read *The Age of Reason* in the light of this political objective. We note in chapter 1 adumbrations of Paine's correlation of religion and politics in his earliest work, and particularly in chapter 2 indicate the ways in which his controversy with Burke served as a transitional stage to his writings on Scripture. In chapter 3 we discuss various previous biblical criticism, mentioned by Paine or available to him either directly or indirectly; and we address certain now outmoded thoughts and beliefs, of interest to Paine, that had accumulated in massive tomes of scriptural commentary and exegesis since the Reformation. In chapter 4 we detail those features of this substantial body of authoritative teaching on the Bible that Paine specifically opposed. And in chapter 5 we focus on the four most cogent replies to *The Age of Reason* as an index to how Paine's book was read in its time.

Throughout these chapters, we try to uncover Paine's intention not only by defining the *intellectual context* of his commentary on religion, but also, as the second main purpose of our study, by discovering what might be called the *personal pretext* for *The Age of Reason:* Paine's struggle for authority. Authority was a central issue of Paine's day, as the continual references to it in *Common Sense* and as the American Revolution itself certainly indicate. In England, as well, the issue was hardly latent, as is evident in Samuel Johnson's observation that many rules of society are merely "the arbitrary edicts of legislators, authorized only by themselves."[5] If in England and America the Whig party was split internally over whether or not to defend or to criticize the ruling order, so too in France was the Jacobin network.[6] In France, the third culture influential on and addressed in Paine's commentaries, authority was, in fact, such a vexing issue that individual attempts to negotiate a political position between the monarchy and the mob were indeed precarious. For example, the Marquis de Lafayette, whom Paine knew personally, was branded as a traitor by royalists and radicals alike.[7] While participating in this overt religio-political struggle as described in his narratives, however, Paine was also engaging in a personal struggle to achieve and assert the authority of his own voice.

On the surface, in his self-declared role as political debater and propagandist, Paine presented himself as a self-made spokesman, without any personal attribution of social place or special learning other than that intrinsic to a proper personal character informed by the divine laws of nature. This strategy, with hardly a change of style, point of view, or person, was featured in his role as political disputant in *Common Sense* and *Rights of Man* as well as religious disputant and biblical interpreter in *The Age of Reason.* He attacked the Bible and the churches based on it, just as he had struck at the English government in his debate with Burke: "on the spot where its principles were still in full operation."[8] Paine aroused great public feeling on both political and religious matters because these concerns were in the forefront of late eighteenth-century attention and could be engaged in high dramatic moments.

But if such moments were dramatic, so were the leading actors in them. These actors assumed a theatrical posture, a role; that is, as Richard Sennett observed, public behavior and speech such as theirs were actions "at a distance from the self." Participating within the tradition of *theatrum mundi,* they and their eighteenth-century peers, consciously or unconsciously, construed their social life in aesthetic terms that, as Sennett documents, identified everyone as actors in the theater of society, where belief and illusion merged.[9] It is not surprising that, as we will see, both Burke and Paine readily resorted to imagery derived from the stage to describe these dramatic events or to impugn the spectacle of each other's performance. Whereas Paine presented himself as a rebellious sectarian, a vulgarian spokesman who thought and acted quite on his own, his equally theatrical adversaries assumed the role of established authority figures who could easily defend the eminent domain of church and state, of Western civilization itself. Whereas Paine claimed to be free from the contamination of arcane scriptural authority, he, in fact, was not as innocent of this knowledge as he declared. Of course, the guise of his emancipation from "the authority of the dead" and of his sole dependence on "reason and principle," "reason and philosophy" (1:252, 4, 467), was useful to him. Not only did this posture help him avoid charges of plagiarism or corruption by previous skeptical thought already deemed unacceptable, but it also identified him as an original, whose authority derived directly from a singular reading of self-evident verity with the "universal order of things" (1:23). Performance was everything, a theatrical voice that gave Paine an identity; but if at one level this performance was founded on intellectual conviction, it was, on another level, also founded on personal conflict, as seems endemic to most struggles for authority.

Paine's contention with authority probably began in his adolescent years, the usual time for its onset. Although one of his most informed biographers suggests that Paine "mentions his father, Joseph, with great affection,"[10] these references, all in passing, occurred late in his life, by which time the ceaselessly revisionary activity of memory generally reassesses one's youthful experiences. It is not necessary to document conclusively that young Paine harbored if not overt, then subtle, resentments concerning the authority of his father, for whom he worked as an apprentice staymaker off and on until he was twenty years old; we need only recall Paine's evident discontent with staymaking and, as well, gather how likely it was that as an adolescent he should have resented paternal control over him.[11]

There is, moreover, a clue to such an undercurrent in Paine's scheme for a progressive tax on landed income (1:437–39). This tax would strike at the heart of patriarchal control of aristocratic families, especially as perpetuated by the mechanism of primogeniture. But this tax would, as well, strike at the heart of paternal authority in working-class families because its revenue would be used in various ways, according to Paine's plan, to assure the financial independence of working-class children.[12]

Pertinent, too, in detecting autobiographical traces in Paine's resistance to authority, is his "adolescent" cry in *Rights of Man* that "every age and generation must be as free to act for itself, *in all cases,* ·as the ages and the generation which preceded it" (1:251). At sixteen, Paine had sought to escape from his father's shop and signed to join a privateer, a dubious venture from which *with distant hindsight* he was gladly spared by his father's affectionate remonstrance. The story of Paine's subsequent signing with still another ship captain cannot be satisfactorily substantiated, but the first episode is sufficient to suggest a certain understandable discomfort in working under the dominion of his father.

And what of Paine's early renunciation of Quaker beliefs? Paine always mentioned his father in relation to devout Quaker beliefs, and even when late in life he spoke of how his father's beliefs led to his own good moral instruction and useful learning, he could not avoid mentioning the limits it placed on his education. Paine's break from this patrimony of Quaker doctrine and the more severe break from established Christian dogma carried with it an undercurrent of his resistance to paternal authority, his generational need to "be as free to act for" himself as perhaps, in Paine's imagination, his father had once been. In any event, we see evidence of this personal element in Paine's assault on patriarchy throughout his career: on King George III in *Common Sense,* on aristocratic Edmund Burke in *Rights of Man*, and on priests, clerics, and theologians in *The Age of Reason.*[13] All were paternal authority figures in their time, and all were deposed by Paine.

Even the Christian God, the Father, was deposed by Paine. In *The Age of Reason* he noted that he "revolted at the recollection of what [he] had heard" about redemption by the death of the Son of God: "It was making God Almighty act like a passionate man who killed His son when He could not revenge Himself in any other way" (1:497). Paine "revolted" in a double sense; he became ill over and resisted generational filiacide. He opposed the despotic control of a young generation by an old one, whose representatives vested themselves in the guise of patriarchal kingship, aristocracy, or priestcraft. As indicated in his declaration in *Rights of Man* that "every age and generation must be as free to act for itself, *in all cases,* as the ages and the generation which preceded it," sons must revolt against such paternal authority, even commit regicide or parricide if necessary, as the second part of *Rights* suggests. [14] And Paine indeed revolted, assailing King George, then Burke, then all establishment theologians, in his effort to save his generation from intellectual filiacide, to free humanity from the patriarchal tyranny of a state in conspiracy with the church.

Paine, however, achieves his own voice, his own authority, by this very process of opposition to established father figures, and this relationship is precarious and paradoxical in nature. [15] It is precarious because the perception of authority is always "a process of interpretive power," so that "the sentiments of authority lie in the eye of the beholder," who experiences both "fear and regret" in trying to penetrate the "secret the authority [figure] possesses." [16] It is paradoxical because identity, when arrived at through a strategy of opposition, only manages an illusion of break and separation. Actually the boundary between the two remains blurred and fluid. In other words, "the very act of rejecting authority can be so constructed that a person feels tied to the person he or she is rejecting." [17] Paine's authority is always grounded on the very authority it deposes, with the result that his voice is little more than a theatrical performance that (as we will see) paradoxically reenacts the maneuvers of deposed authority figures, whose own sovereignty has likewise been the effect of a performance. One telling example will now suffice.

In *Common Sense* and the *Crisis* papers, Paine makes several allusions to book 4 of John Milton's *Paradise Lost,* a work well known in the eighteenth century, when a number of studies of Milton appeared, including one in Samuel Johnson's *Lives of the Poets* (1779–81). Besides referring to "Lucifer in his revolt" and "the ruins of the bowers of paradise," Paine recalls the scene (*Paradise Lost* 4:799–809) where Satan creates a delusive dream for Eve by whispering in her ear while she sleeps (1:5, 28, 59). Paine's most direct reference occurs in an accurate quotation from *Paradise Lost* (4:98–99): "Never can true reconcilement grow where wounds of deadly hate have pierced so deep" (1:23). The course of these allusions bears some attention.

Throughout *Common Sense* and the *Crisis* papers, Paine associates King George III with demonic forces. It is he, like all kings and their minions, who is Luciferian in having deluded mankind and destroyed the possibility of human happiness on earth, the paradise regained to which Paine's millennial impulse is so intensely dedicated. [18] Monarchical authority is no more than a perversion of the universal design of the Deity, which for Paine is everywhere intrinsically manifest in nature and the human mind. However, in the direct quotation from *Paradise Lost,* it is rebellious Paine and other revolutionary American colonists, not the king, who are associated with Satan. In Milton's work this quoted passage occurs just prior to Satan's firm resolution not to seek forgiveness, but to nurture his hate and to assail "Heav'n's King," as if he were a son rebelling against a father. Paine applies this same resoluteness to himself, and in the process identifies with the fierceness of Satanic rebellion against divine authority.

This momentary alliance between the speaker and Satan anticipates Paine's inclination toward regicide in the second part of *Rights of Man,* as if he were revengefully inverting the doctrine of the death of the son (filiacide) at the hands of God, the Father, heaven's King, specifically remarked later in *The Age of Reason.* But this alliance also anticipates a dilemma in Paine's own performance: that his pretentious voice of authority (every bit as dramatic as Satan's in *Paradise Lost*) cannot separate itself ultimately from the authority it deposes. Sometimes, as in Paine's example, intense criticism is a form of identification.[19]

In fact, Paine's voice is authorized only through the enablement of its opposition to established authority figures. It has no other reason to exist. Beneath the maneuvers of the theatrical performance of Paine's disembodied voice, the illusion of its break from an opposed authority, the delusion of self-fathering, gives way to the paradox of mimicry: the appropriation and reenactment of—a mode of identification with—that very same deposed authority. This stage-effect interests us in our study as a sign of the conflicted personal pretext underlying Paine's ostensible intellectual intentions.

A subterranean anxiety belies Paine's *obiter dicta* presented as *ex cathedra* proclamations, as if his covert identification with the victims of his Satanic parricidal and regicidal impulses harbors (in some profound sense) suicidal implications buried deep within, where they undermine his declaration of personal independence.[20] His oracular representation of himself as a self-made spokesman, without any attribution of place or learning other than that intrinsic to a proper character influenced by the divinely informed laws of nature, is not firm. In fact, this alleged origin, this transferral of authority to a remote "reason and principle," is known only through its manifest representation, the performing voice of Paine asserting this infinitely distant (and so absent) priority to its own speech. *Representation* is the key word here. The eighteenth century may be known as the Enlightenment, the Neoclassical Age, and (after Paine's title) the Age of Reason, but it could, as we note in chapter 1, just as well be referred to as the Age of Representation. Among public figures, at least, so very much was theatrical in this age of diplomacy, not only in political affairs but also in social manners.

If *The Age of Reason* was not quite the original book Paine proclaimed it to be, it was by no means a mere redaction of arguments prevalent in his cultural milieux[21] any more than it was a mere expression of his anxious quest for authority. As if reflecting the internal division of its author's authority between evident dependence and declared autonomy, *The Age of Reason* is a startling synthesis of his intellectual context and his personal pretext, on the one hand, and of genuine profound insight, on the other. For a number of Paine's ideas concerning Scripture, ideas only dimly understood in his time, would become major and guiding principles in biblical interpretation during the early decades of the nineteenth century, and later. Paine anticipated subsequent efforts to demystify Scripture,[22] to differentiate primary from deutero commentary in the two Testaments,[23] to reconstruct the various patristic interpretations of Scripture that specifically instated ecclesiastical and civil government,[24] and to scrutinize generally how actions based on religious belief coincide with political behavior,[25] among other twentieth-century theological interests. In the light of such latter-day concerns, *The Age of Reason* is a prescient book as well as a representative one of its time. The intellectual context and the authorial pretext of its representative identity, however, remain the two primary concerns of our investigation of Paine's remarkable book.

1

Young Paine and
Biblical Authority

Whatever the detail and wealth of biographical information on Paine throughout his career, and especially in the dramatic times of his American and French experience, there is almost nothing about him as a living person. He wrote letters, and they have survived. He made strong impressions on friends and associates, and their testimony has survived. He expressed himself directly and even personally in his writings; indeed, he put *himself* at the forefront of attention. One senses energy, urgency, confidence. And yet, except for his later *Letter to Washington* (1796), with its bitter sense of betrayal by a former friend, there is no presence of Thomas Paine, the "person," in all of that record that has survived him: no intimate disclosures, no variable and suggestive touches of a man as he was, little or nothing of signs of affection or hate or resentment. He seems, as far as the official record reflects, not to have passed through any great personal crisis, for all his effective use of the term *crisis* in a series of eloquent papers.

To be sure, he suffered from poverty and made his way to America in 1774, with hardly a shilling in his pocket. He was imprisoned for ten months in 1794, and nearly met the guillotine. He had on occasion to flee for his life. Even so, whoever was that person Thomas Paine who effected such changes in the way many people felt about their government and about their times remains a remote, even chill and slightly forbidding, figure.

This distance is a characteristic of other prominent figures of Paine's milieu as well. As we mentioned in the Introduction, his time might be aptly described not only as the Age of Reason or the Enlightenment or the Neoclassical Age, but also as the Age of Representation. It was a time when people believed, as a southern contemporary of Paine typically phrased it, that "man is a Sociable animal"[1] seeking happiness through human interaction, or civil covenants; so it was also a time when public appearance, externality, was emphasized, a time of diplomacy managed by negotiating social voices representing a position or an image and revealing a speaker's personal interior only indirectly. Benjamin Franklin's autobiography, an amalgamation of such negotiating voices, is a good case in point, and present-day scholars readily contend over the personae, the rhetorical strategies, the management and accuracy of detail, and even the actual beliefs of Franklin in this ambiguous work. Thomas Jefferson's autobiography, usually of much less interest to these same critics, is, nonetheless, another case in point; only the outer lineament of an impersonal self is autobiographically presented to the world by Jefferson in a portrait of an author knowable solely through a public history paradoxically written by the unseen private self he does not reveal.[2]

It would seem, accordingly, that the religious principles and beliefs of such a "represented" person would have the same formidable and distant character as the represented Thomas Paine himself. And so they do. There is little if any religious feeling (if "feeling" it can be called) in Paine's religious writings. His expressions of religious idea and conviction are of the same form and mode as are his political convictions. In Paine's opinion, the rhetoric of one is virtually interchangeable with that of the other, and as we will contend, indeed Paine understood the aim of the former to be virtually identical with that of the latter.

The reason for this association is clear. Paine was primarily interested in society and politics, the workings of human thought and action in the world as it was in his time and as it might be in the future. But religion was a most significant and pervasive authority in that world of society and politics. In his desire to further the movement of humanity toward a secular millennium, Paine sought to locate all the impediments to human advancement toward a better world, and *eventually* he focused on established religion as a fundamental culprit. To the end of exposing the pseudoauthority of established religion as a mainstay of the social and political malaise of his time, Paine devoted his best energies late in his life.

Of course, to depose the authority of established religion Paine had to present himself as an authority on religion, especially on the Bible. The subtle features of this assumption of authoritative voice concern us throughout this study, but first we need to attend to the issue of what can be documented about Paine's knowledge of the Bible before he wrote *The Age of Reason.*

Paine knew the Bible during his boyhood in a pious Quaker household. "My father being of the Quaker profession," he confided in *The Age of Reason,* "it was my good fortune to have an exceedingly good moral education, and a tolerable stock of useful learning. Though I went to the

grammar school, I did not learn Latin, not only because I had no inclination to learn languages, but because of the objection the Quakers have
against the books in which the language is taught. But this did not prevent
me," Paine concluded, "from being acquainted with the subjects of all the
Latin books used in the school." We know almost nothing else about
Paine's early schooling and religious training except his further remark
that he "may presume [to] assert . . . that the Quakers have no priests, no
bells—and they are remarkable for the care of the poor of their society"
(1:496).

His exposure to the Bible was doubtless augmented during his early
manhood, when he taught English for some months in 1766 in an acad-
emy maintained by Daniel Noble (1729–83), a Baptist minister. Unpopu-
lar in this post and not recommended by Noble as a suitable candidate for
ordination, Paine (if traditional accounts are reliable in this matter)
engaged in itinerant preaching during 1766 and 1767. According to
Francis Oldys, Paine's first and not always accurate biographer, Paine
"determined to persevere in his purpose, without regular orders. And so
he preached in Moorfields, and in other popular places in England, as he
was urged by his necessities, or directed by his spirit. The text, which so
emphatically inculcates, *meddle not with them that are given to change,*
we may easily suppose, he superficially explained, or seldom enforced."[3]

Although his adherence to his early Quaker training seems to have
been brief, it not only made the Bible familiar to him, but also may have
provided him with an unacknowledged authorization to speak about the
Bible, especially later in life, when he needed to find some such enablement for assailing Scripture itself. The Quaker doctrine of the Inward
Light, "the true Light, which lighteth every man" (John 1:9), may have
imparted a special sense of the individual that, however unexamined,
possibly continued to empower, even legitimatize, Paine's later proto-
Emersonian voice, particularly when speaking authoritatively against the
authority of established religion. This issue is more complex than the
possible influence of the doctrine of the Inward Light on Paine's writings,
as we will see, but it is important to acknowledge the very likely role of
this Quaker doctrine as one hidden wellspring of Paine's voice.[4]

While an itinerant preacher, Paine was apparently actively thinking
over various religious beliefs. A certain Reverend Jacob Duchè, a Sweden-
borgian sympathizer and in 1776 a chaplain to the American Congress,
wrote to Paine on a subject of evidently mutual interest. "I never could
understand the doctrine of the Trinity," Duchè wrote to Paine on 18
December 1767, "& had an irreconcilable aversion to the Systematical
Notion of atonement & satisfaction. A wrathful God whose anger could

only be appeased by the blood of His own Son pour'd out in behalf of Sinners always appear'd to me next to blasphemous."[5] Later in *The Age of Reason,* as noted in our Introduction and later in our Conclusion, Paine would echo this observation and specifically decry the pathology of a divine patriarchal father who requires the death of his son.

Beyond these few clues, there is little information available about Paine's specific knowledge of theological and biblical matters. And Paine's biographers have been willing to pass over, with only a spare sentence or two, the matter of Paine's religious beliefs during the first thirty-seven years of his life. There is, however, more to be said on the subject. Paine arrived in America on 30 November 1774, with a letter of introduction in hand from Benjamin Franklin, and it is in America that more clues to Paine's knowledge of Scripture emerge, particularly in *Common Sense* (1776).

In *Common Sense* Paine's most considerable use of the Bible occurs in a passage arguing against concepts of kingship and monarchy. He quotes nearly the whole of chapters 8 through 12 of 1 Samuel, the scriptural condemnation of the Jews' "idolatrous" demand for a king and the reluctant submission of the prophet Samuel to their desire (1:11–12). This direct, accurate quotation makes the point that the Old Testament Israelites went against the will of God and thereafter suffered the oppression of kingship, which in turn led to the division of the kingdom into two, to the subsequent fall of Jerusalem, and to the Captivity in Babylon. The message for Paine's American audience was doubtless clear, perhaps specifically to those who still carried in their minds a sense of America's New Israelite destiny or of the jeremiads warning of the possible failure of this mission.[6] Paine implies that to fulfill its destiny the New World must not repeat the historical pattern of the biblical Israelites.

Both in their reliance on Scripture and in their rhetorical manner, *Common Sense* and the *Crisis* papers seem to support the tradition concerning Paine's itinerant preaching. The biblical analogies and examples he uses in these works appear to flow with ease from a mind accustomed to thinking in scriptural terms. The American colonists, Paine typically notes, were "separating [them]selves from the cities of Sodom and Gomorrah," whereas in contrast, in submitting to an autocratic government the English people "have shaven [their] own head" in the same manner that "Samson [had]. . . told the secret . . . and wantonly thrown away the locks" (1:83, 148). The English oppressors have been driven "like Pharaoh, to unpitied miseries" (1:161).

This convenient, even ready manner of association occurs as well in Paine's routine references to the colonists as benefiting from "the gracious hand of Heaven." Because King George III is "a Herod of uncommon malice," Paine comments, it is "the will of God [that] has parted" the colonists from the king. "America [is] of too much value in the scale of Providence to be cast like a pearl before swine," Paine writes in echo of Scripture, for "the country was the gift of heaven, and God alone is their Lord and Sovereign" (1:118–20). Paine's quotations and references in these and other instances recall a standard, conventional reliance on Scripture in his time for the evidence necessary to illustrate an argument.

But much more is involved in such moments as these in *Common Sense* and the *Crisis* papers than merely the rhetorical management of biblical allusions designed to elicit certain emotions in an audience long exposed to a tradition of such usage. Also important within this tradition is the emphatic association of religious discourse and political agenda, not only from the Puritans onward in the New World, but in England as well; for Paine was sure from the outset of the Revolution that "*religious and political principles*" are joined together in mutual support of each other (1:77).[7] In *Common Sense* he does not pause over this connection; dedicated to calling for a declaration of independence, he has little time in this work to probe such matters. As will be evident in our study, however, Paine would forcefully return to this matter nearly twenty years later, when in *The Age of Reason* he would observe how this very connection, when perverted, vexes the advancement of humanity.

In *Common Sense* Paine anticipates his eventual position when he observes that "in the early ages of the world, according to the scripture chronology"—this phrase "scripture chronology" would become prominent later (1:524–25)—"there were no kings; the consequence of which was, there were no wars; it is the pride of kings which throws mankind into confusion" (1:9). To be sure, the reproach of kings here and in *The Forester's Letters* (1776) is meant, as are Jefferson's anathemas of King George III in the Declaration of Independence, to have a contemporary edge and bearing. Nonetheless, Paine's point (expressed in Miltonic terms) is that monarchy recapitulates (as it were) Satan's subversion of the harmony of creation: "The palaces of kings are built upon the ruins of the bowers of paradise"; "If the history of the creation and the history of kings be compared together the result will be this—that God hath made a world, and kings have robbed him of it" (1:4–5, 2:79). To eliminate monarchy would be to restore an Edenic feature of God's original world.

A crucial moment in this pattern of association occurs, as we noted, when Paine resorts to the authority of the Old Testament, specifically to the long quotation from 1 Samuel, to deny human authority for any "form of government which so impiously invades the prerogative of heaven"

(1:10); "That the Almighty hath . . . here entered his protest against monarchical government is true, or the scripture is false" (1:12). Paine knows that his audience credits the authority of the Bible without question; for that audience, as his rhetorical manner indicates, scriptural analogy speaks for itself. But Paine's dance around this issue of authority is more subtle than is immediately apparent. It is, in fact, as subtle as have been, in his opinion, the claims of kings to power. *Subtle* is the telling word in Paine's observation that in presenting "the will of the king" under the guise or "formidable shape of an act of parliament" we can see that "the fate of Charles the First hath only made kings more subtle—not more just" (1:9). For Paine, we can surmise, any claim to authority is based on subtlety.

But in 1776, Paine was apparently willing to leave unquestioned the subtleties of scriptural claims to authority, and that latent matter is readily elided for the urgent purposes of his political mission in *Common Sense.* He was not, however, unaware of the problem of the legitimation of his own voice in this pamphlet, a problem he had to negotiate as subtly as he says kings do their own imperious voice. If monarchs, in Paine's opinion, effect their will through the guise of the parliamentary representatives of the people, so too, one must observe, does an author like Paine, who adopts a persona who is anonymous, a mere representative of the "universal" evident in "the cause of America," which is after all "the cause of all mankind" (1:3). The postscript to the introduction of the anonymously published February 1776 edition of *Common Sense* says directly, "Who the author of this production is, is wholly unnecessary to the public, as the object for attention is the *doctrine itself,* not the *man*" (1:4).

The seemingly incidental, even offhand, placement of this comment itself comprises a sleight of hand. Such positioning relegates the comment to the margin of the reader's attention. Yet what it says is disingenuous. It masks the persona's self-attribution of an exemplary, superior degree of rationality that can pierce through the mystification of monarchical politics and established religion. For if the anonymous persona is truly representative of the "we," "us," and "our" with whom he is so fond of identifying,[8] he would be as mystified as the rest of us concerning the self-evident universal cause of America, or what he has to say, to argue, to assert, would already be as self-evident to us as it is to him as merely an indistinguishable and interchangeable member of his community.

But he is not one with that community. In *Common Sense* he readily admits "the inability of moral virtue to govern the world": "[W]ere the impulses of conscience clear, uniform, and irresistibly obeyed, man would need no other law-giver" (1:6, 5). So until such time as this millennial ideal comes into existence, the persona of *Common Sense* must play the governing part. To do so, he merely asserts his position in the same manner as kings, in his opinion, assume the posture of doing the will of the people by "representing" the people as they ought to be. However, given the absence of the reality, the millennial ideal, represented by Paine's persona, there is nothing empirical, documentable, or phenom- enally grounded available to credit him; his license is based on an absence, nothing at all, and so he must resort to self-assertion, mere language, fortified by the presumably self-evident and unquestionable divine verity of Scripture, which (paradoxically) nonetheless "expressly disapproves of government by kings" (1:10). In this way the persona of *Common Sense* deposes monarchs and, at the same time, in his own performance of voice, achieves his identity negatively (disassociation) and positively (asso- ciation): negatively, by defining himself through opposition so that he is enabled and "embodied" by what he opposes; positively, by confiscating the *subtle* manner of asserted sovereignty attributed to kings, whom he accuses of "jesuitically" managing language (1:19).

Paine's mimicry of the arrogation of authority he attributes to kings is not only suggested in assertions reminiscent of magisterial proclamations and buttressed by biblical analogies that speak for themselves without question; it also includes a subtle appropriation of "regal authority" founded on "the seal of divine authority" (1:27, 15). For even though the anonymous author does allude throughout *Common Sense* to "the natural rights of all mankind," to "the concern of every man to whom nature hath given the power of feeling," to "the influence of reason and principle," to "the universal order of things," to (in short) "common sense," none of these asserted claims to an empirical, demonstrable, phenomenally ground- ed basis for action is ever explored, and each simply gives way in the discourse proper to a mere reliance on divine scriptural authority. Whether or not this deflection suggests Paine's deliberate accommodation of audience, the *effect* of his procedure, in any event, is one of arrogation of the very divine authorization for kingship that he renounces from the start on presumably self-evident ground.

Authorially identified simply as "Common Sense," Paine declares in the thirteenth and final *Crisis* paper (19 April 1776): "It was the cause of America that made me an author. The force with which it struck my mind . . . made it impossible for me, feeling as I did, to be silent" (1:235). There is truth in Paine's statement; for his previous authorship in England shows no special talent for writing. Nevertheless, in this statement, the displacement of personal motive to representative cause is of greater signif- icance. In seeming to abdicate individual authority, the author subtly reigns, just as he does in *Common Sense*. His alleged representative self in effect re-presents his individual voice; he merely disguises this doctrinaire voice by claiming that it emanates from the parliamentary-like power of his community:

> So far as my endeavors could go, they have all been directed to conciliate the affections, unite the interests, and draw and keep the mind of the country together. . . . I have avoided all places of profit or office . . . kept myself at a distance from all parties . . . and even disregarded all private and inferior concerns: and when we take into view the great work which we have gone through . . . we ought to feel, the just importance of it. (1:234–35)

The tension created by contradiction in this passage is worth noting. The slippage from "I" to "we" almost mutes any sense of personal motive, but finally a discrepancy becomes evident in the light of the authorial claim of mere representation. For if the speaker is truly personally disinterested (avoiding and disregarding "at a distance"), if the speaker is nearly a disembodied hagiographic voice of the community of "we," how is it that, unlike that community, he was so much "at a distance" that he was exempt from the problem "we" had, the problem of unreconciled affections, disunited interests, and disordered mind? Does not his exemption from this discord, his distant position, his (as it were) Parnassian vision, elevate him above "us"? Does he here not present himself with a kinglike supremacy, at once the bestower of social order and the expression of the will of the people, were they capable of realizing it?

Paine's slippage from "I" to "we" may be meant as a form of subtle association, a populist attempt to merge individual voice and communal identity. But within the same passage this slippage also curiously reasserts the gap between "I" and "we"; for the intimated magisterial prerogative of an exemplary persona, who relies on the self-evident verity of scriptural analogy as if it were "the seal of divine authority" for his imperious pronouncements, seeks to impose order over social chaos. Read this way, the coalescence of "I" and "we" in this passage ironically to some degree recovers the sense of the royal "we" used by monarchs.

This paradoxical abdication and reclamation of kingly authority occurs in the next paragraph, the penultimate one of this *Crisis* paper: "Independence always appeared to me practical and probable, provided the sentiment of the country could be formed and held to the object" (1:235). Again the author conveys a sense of distance from the community; he sees, as if from a prospect or inspired by the Inward Light, more than is seen by the community, the sentiment of which needs to "be formed." The author evasively deletes the agent to this passive voice construction. To be formed by whom? The answer lies in the antecedent, virtually parallel construction in the same sentence: it "appeared to me" and "could be formed" by *me*.

Throughout both *Common Sense* and the *Crisis* papers, Paine's voice claims to be at once passive and active, disinterested and interested, present and distant, average and special. An anonymously communal representative "we" as well as a divinely envisioned regal "I" who echoes the regal use of "we," this persona concludes with an equally double-voiced claim, problematically suspended between the personal and the communal, about the merits of its narration: "I have likewise added something to the reputation of literature, by freely and disinterestedly employing it in the great cause of mankind, and showing that there may be genius without prostitution" (1:235).

Paine's denial of any craft or art is itself a very artful and crafty enterprise, one designed to suggest that the "genius" of the author is not only a *passive representation* of the community as a whole but also an *active presentation* of the new man with a new style, both prophesying a new community that would become a model for the rest of the world. Although Paine says of kings that "how a race of men came into the world so exalted above the rest, and distinguished like some new species, is worth inquiring into" (1:9), the issue of his own representation of the new American type is elided. He wrote *Common Sense* and the *Crisis* papers as someone professing his lack of experience, as someone only empowered by the enterprise itself; but at the same time he presents himself, through the performance of his oracular language alone, as someone professing his singular destiny to be a biblically authorized spokesman for nearly everything that the American cause declared in the way of rights and freedoms of its people, especially as defined against a background of the tyranny of kings, including those "sullen-tempered Pharaoh[s] of England" (1:25). Finally, however, such a maneuver amounts only to a form of subtle self-authorization, asserted through a tradition of apparently biblically sanctioned language, similar to the contrived self-empowerment of the very monarchs Paine exposed and deposed. By relying on scriptural authority and thereby mimicking the subtlety of monarchic self-authorization in his own performance, Paine inadvertently damages his own argument. If his exposure of the corrupt alliance between established religion and monarchical power is valid, then his "democratic" appropriation of their authority contaminates and subverts his claim for the "new man." For when Paine rehabilitates the very same patterns of the past he ostensibly rejects, the new man he calls for, and in some sense typifies, fails to show "that there may be genius without prostitution."

Paine's problematical location of authority in a repudiation of the past that simultaneously resorts to traditional scriptural authority and rearticulates traditional monarchical strategies of authorization, one could speculate, might have been reinforced (not caused) by his lack of skill in citing legal, philosophical, and political spokesmen out of the past. The Bible notwithstanding, the secular commentators he did cite were those of recent and contemporary document and reasoning; his support for the Revolution was never derived from the noble statements on human rights, the powers of kings and government, or the rules of adjusting difference between people. His guides were in every case the statements in immediate thought and discussion, and they could not protect him from the sort of pitfall we have described.

At the end of the Revolutionary War, Paine was most adept in managing a style and rhetoric suitable to public contention and particularly serviceable in treating a contemporary issue in all its immediacy. When he engaged in a debate with the Abbé Raynal concerning the rights of people to revolt, he relied on events such as Washington's defeat of the British at Trenton and on recently published tracts that he brought to bear on the subject at hand. But Paine's apparent reliance on the empirical, the demonstrable, the phenomenally grounded, is only chimerical and always yields in the discourse proper of *Common Sense* and the *Crisis* papers to an implicit reliance on divine scriptural authority or to an implicit reliance on replicated monarchical strategies of subtle self-authorization. This always formed and always de-formed coalescence of the local and the universal, of the self and the community, constitutes Paine's method, as he well stated himself: "My principle is universal. My attachment is to all the world, and not to any particular part, and what I advance is right, no matter where or who it comes from" (1:146).

"What I advance is right, no matter where or who it comes from," whether that be some external source such as Scripture or some internal source such as the self, where inspiration is like an experience of the Inward Light. Paradoxically, whenever Paine claims through dogmatic assertion, through the mere performance of oracular language, the compliance of his particular beliefs with universal principles, he instinctively seeks a hermetically sealed self-empowerment as his ground for warrant, "no matter where or who it comes from." Such autonomy, however, remains elusive, a mere fantasy, as is suggested by Paine's subtle confiscation of the strategies of his magisterial opponent.

This peculiar problem of an authority simultaneously constructed (re-presented) and de-constructed in relation to the connection between religious and political principles presents a fascinating puzzle throughout Paine's writings, but provides a special site of interest in *The Age of Reason*. In this later work, the main focus of our study, Paine will refute the supremacy of Scripture itself because it had been used to legitimate kingship and monarchies—a stance that certainly undermines his use of the Bible in *Common Sense* and the *Crisis* papers as an authority deauthor-izing kingship and monarchies and, even more significantly, as a legitima-tion for his own exemplary voice and identity. To explore the implications of this development, we now turn our attention to the background of *The Age of Reason*.

2

The Burke-Paine Controversy
As Prelude

The Reverend Richard Price (1723–91) was a Unitarian minister who had written *Observations on the Nature of Civil Liberty, the Principles of Civil Government, and the Justice and Policy of the War with America* (1777), a strongly pro-American work. For this publication he had been awarded an honorary degree from Yale University and had been invited by the American Congress to come to the United States and accept citizenship.[1] Of still greater importance was a sermon the Reverend Price delivered on 4 November 1789 to what was called the Revolution Society, a sermon published that year as *A Discourse on the Love of Our Country*.

Price spoke in the aftermath of the opening of the French Revolution, and his discourse contains matter supporting the French cause. His sermon, however, more generally condemns most of the governments "now in the world" as "little better than contrivances for enabling the few to oppress the many," as "usurpations of the rights of man," a phrase that would become emphatic in the debate a few months ahead. Such rights as are guaranteed to British citizens are not, Price maintained, fully recognized in British political life; of a certainty religious freedom cannot exist so long as civil freedom is unrealized and ineffective. With this belief in mind, Price offered an exultant welcome to the idea of revolution: "Tremble all ye oppressors of the world! Take warning all ye supporters of slavish governments, and slavish hierarchies!" A new day was dawning, when there would arise in Europe "a blaze that lays despotism in ashes, and warms and illuminates Europe!"[2]

Price's sermon, issued early in December, soon became a best-seller with printings in Paris, Dublin, and Boston. Edmund Burke read it when he returned to London in mid-January 1790. On the night of his arrival, he immediately began making notes for a public answer to "this spiritual doctor of politics."[3] Presumably Burke's published reply reflects his initial reaction, for it records the same concern he expressed at that time in a letter written to a friend: namely, that there was already in England "a considerable party . . . proceeding systematically" to the destruction of the constitution and the church. Burke knew that Dissenters like Price and also Joseph Priestley were active and influential, and that the political movement forming a subtle campaign against the established church had suspicious French connections.[4]

These suspicions were heightened after 17 January 1790, little more than a month after Price's discourse appeared in print. On that date Paine, in Paris, wrote Burke a letter containing an excerpt from one of Jefferson's letters to Paine. This excerpt suggested that the French Revolution was not an event confined to France but "certainly," Paine announced, "a Forerunner to other Revolutions in Europe." This letter no doubt further confirmed Burke's conviction that the French Revolution evidenced a systematic and diabolic plan to spread a false philosophy designed to destroy the established European order—indeed, civilization itself.[5]

If Paine and Burke were never intimate friends, neither were they mere acquaintances. While Paine was in England in 1787 and 1788 to demonstrate his model for a suspension bridge,[6] he developed (according to Thomas Copeland) a fairly close relationship with Burke. Burke wrote to John Wilkes in August 1788: "I am just going to dine with the Duke of Portland, in company with the great American, Paine, whom I take with me."[7] Paine was at this time on a week-long visit to Beaconsfield, Burke's country estate, and his introduction to the duke helped Paine find support for his bridge. Later, while Paine was in Yorkshire superintending the construction of an iron model of his bridge, Burke paid him a visit at the ironworks. In the succeeding months of 1788, Burke seems to have welcomed Paine and to have discussed political affairs with him. Paine wrote to one of his American correspondents, "I am in pretty close intimacy with the heads of the opposition—the Duke of Portland, Mr. Fox and Mr. Burke. . . . I am in as elegant style of acquaintance here as any American that ever came over" (2:1276).

What attracted Paine to Burke remains a mystery. Paine was aware of Burke's useful and powerful connections, but beyond this matter of expediency Paine must have also admired Burke's earlier efforts, while he was a member of Parliament, to get his government to treat the American colonies more wisely. As Paine later noted in his preface to the English edition of *The Rights of Man:* "From the part Mr. Burke took in the American Revolution, it was natural that I should consider him a friend to mankind; and as our acquaintance commenced on that ground, it would have been more agreeable to me to have cause to continue in that opinion than to change it" (1:244). Perhaps Paine was sincere in this comment, perhaps disingenuous; whatever the truth of the matter, his sketchy portrait of Burke in this passage is problematical, especially in light of Burke's political behavior prior to and during the Revolutionary War.

Burke indeed spoke for the repeal of the Stamp Act in 1766, when Benjamin Franklin and others testified before Parliament against the measure; but, when the repeal succeeded on 18 March 1766, Burke also supported on that same day the successful passage of the Declaratory Act, which unequivocally reaffirmed the complete constitutional power of the British government to legislate any laws pertaining to the American colonies, including taxes. Nor did Burke's position change in the 1770s; although he stressed moderation and conciliation in lieu of the ruthless exercise of imperial power, he never questioned the constitutionality of Britain's complete dominion over the colonies.

This dominion was most assuredly questioned by Paine, who (if he knew about them at all) could only have also thought of Burke's arguments calling merely for the limitation of crown patronage in the 1780s as beside the point. In short, Burke's defense of various reforms was always restricted by his unshakable conviction that traditional political, social, and religious institutions represented a collective human wisdom not to be gainsaid by any impetuous emotion of the present moment. What could have been more inimical to Paine's own virtually millennial position in the late 1780s, when he was enjoying Burke's attention?

Perhaps Paine had initially responded to Burke's elevated popular reputation in the colonies, as "America's greatest friend in England, after his speech 'On Reconciliation with America' (1775)." [8] In their enthusiastic celebration of the repeal of the Stamp Act, the colonists virtually overlooked the passage of the Declaratory Act, not to mention Burke's support of it. Perhaps Burke's association with Whig supporters of the marquis of Rockingham, who also seemed inclined toward conciliation with the colonies and modification of royal power, figured in Paine's original assessment of Burke. Perhaps Burke's penchant for mixed discourse, at once integrating Whig and Tory rhetoric,[9] allowed Paine to hear what he wanted to hear, as he seems to have done with Lafayette.

Or perhaps Paine's attachment to Burke expressed some deep personal need, some unconscious regard for an accomplished father figure of sorts. Pertinent to this possibility is the puzzling detail that Paine readily submitted to Burke's authoritative scrutiny the correspondence he was having with certain Frenchmen on the subject of peace, whereas at the same time he assumed his customary position of personal authority in his correspondence with such leading American figures as George Washington, Benjamin Franklin, James Madison, John Jay, and John Adams.

Nevertheless, even if Paine might have been blinded by the received colonial representation of Burke and even if some undisclosed personal need might have informed his pursuit of Burke's favor, it could not have been long before he detected profound differences between them. Nor, as someone who during the previous decade had spoken in the voice of the new self-authorized man, could he have been completely comfortable deferring to Burke as an authority figure.

Whether the result of misinformation, expediency, friendship, or desire for a father figure, Paine's unlikely relationship with Burke could not last. It readily ruptured shortly after the appearance of Price's discourse. While in France in 1790, Paine had supplied Burke with news of local events, and in one unguarded letter he doctrinairely declared, "How much good the propagation of French opinions [would be] throughout Europe and England." Burke was incensed, as Paine might well have guessed by then, and Burke broke "off all intercourse with Payne."[10]

In January 1790, Burke began to write an answer to Price's *Discourse* to warn England of what might come to pass. "In reality," as he noted at the time, "my object was not France, in the first instance, but this Country."[11] By the time Paine returned to London from Paris around 1 April, he was already aware of what Burke was preparing, and he was resolved to answer Burke's *Reflections,* as it would be known, when it should appear. Now he was shy of making a friendly and close contact: "I am so out of humour with Mr. Burke," he wrote on 14 April, "with respect to the French Revolution . . . that I have not called on him upon my arrival."[12] But on 6 May Paine sent a note (missing) to Burke which said "that upon the condition that the French Revolution should not be a subject . . . [he] would call upon him the next day."[13] The agreement to continue to meet, albeit also to avoid the topic of the revolution in France, seems somehow to have continued well into the summer of 1790.[14] This association between the two men must have been rather strained at this point, although Paine was obviously very reluctant to end it.

Within a year this strain apparently reached its limit; the contention between Burke and Paine could no longer be contained. Burke now formed his final judgment of Paine; he wrote in a letter to a friend:

He is utterly incapable of comprehending his subject. He has not even a moderate portion of learning of any kind. He has learnd [*sic*] the instrumental part of literature, a style, and a method of disposing his ideas, without having ever made a previous preparation of Study or thinking. . . . Payne possesses nothing more than what a man whose audacity makes him careless of logical consequences, and his total want of honour and morality makes indifferent as to political consequences, may very easily write. . . . The People whom he would corrupt, and who are very corruptible, can very readily comprehend what flatters their vices, and falls in with their ignorance.[15]

Besides the difference of opinion registered in this remark, one also detects Burke's imperious dismissal of Paine's authority as nothing more than an uneducated assertive voice, merely "a style, and a method" morally hollow at their core.

Politics, Religion, and Language: Burke's *Reflections on the Revolution in France*

Burke's *Reflections on the Revolution in France and on the Proceedings of Certain Societies in London Relative to That Event; In a Letter Intended to Have Been Sent to a Gentleman in Paris* was published on 1 November 1790. Selling at five shillings, it was in its time an expensive book. Its length and complexity of argument also limited its likely audience to educated and leisured readers. Nevertheless, it sold seven thousand copies the first week of its sale and twelve thousand within the next three weeks. A French edition sold out in two days, and within months German and Italian translations appeared, followed by reprints of the English edition in Ireland and America in 1791. Within two months *Reflections* had provoked ten pamphlets in reply.[16] Over sixty more were to be published before the war of words ended in silence with the Reign of Terror.

As these statistics suggest, Burke's book strongly influenced British opinion and made the 1790s the arena for a major debate on politics and religion. The specific problematical conjunction itself of politics and religion was not at specific issue at this point in time, but Burke's stark claim that the politics of the revolutionists was founded on atheism became a critical factor in Paine's motivation in *Rights of Man* and his purpose later in *The Age of Reason.*

Burke expressed in grandly moving argument and brilliant rhetoric his fear that the insidious and radical principles set loose in France would spread like a "plague" across Europe, even into England, where there was already an organized band of persons eager to foster and disseminate these radical ideas. There were several core principles to Burke's argument.

First, the French Revolution was a civil war directed against all of Europe, a war "between the partisans of the ancient, civil, moral, and political order of Europe against a sect of fanatical and ambitious atheists which means to change them all."[17] Burke regarded these revolutionists as not "any other than Atheists," a conclusion he affirmed, "I have not lightly formed, or that I can lightly quit."[18] Besides the emotional appeal to his primarily Christian contemporary audience, Burke's allegation that the fomenters of revolution were atheists essentially amounted, in his view, to a denial of any licitness or credit for their political beliefs and partisan behavior.

Indeed, to Burke they seemed almost Satanic in their effort to over-throw the divinely established social order, to "Destroy all Europe." In one of his most eloquent paragraphs, early in *Reflections* Burke echoed Paine's letter of the previous February—"the Revolution in France is cer-tainly a Forerunner to other Revolutions in Europe"[19]—with his own som-ber judgment: "The French Revolution is the most astonishing that has hitherto happened in the world. The most wonderful things are brought about in many instances by means the most absurd and ridiculous, in the most ridiculous modes." And as if sardonically rephrasing Paine's letter, which hailed the revolution for having "the effect of spreading the doctrines . . . in places where other ways it would not be known, and even *that* knowledge will have some effect," Burke concluded: "In viewing this monstrous tragic-comic scene, the most opposite passions necessarily succeed and sometimes mix with each other in the mind: alternate con-tempt and indignation, alternate laughter and tears, alternate scorn and horror."[20]

Burke's second principle was a natural component of the first: there is and must be for humanity a natural moral order that relies on the history and wisdom of the past. This natural moral order has emerged over the centuries by long trial and experience. It has arisen from a human sense of virtue derived from "the constitution of the mind of man." "Our manners, our civilization, and all the good things which are connected with manners and with civilization," Burke further proclaimed, have "depended for ages upon . . . the spirit of a gentleman and the spirit of religion."[21] Here again, Burke relates established religion and the traditional political order, and in this manner he rehabilitates the goal of Reverend Price, whom Burke had scornfully demeaned as a "spiritual doctor of politics." This specific con-junction of contemporary church and state would rankle Paine, who would respond to it obliquely in *Rights of Man* and directly in *The Age of Reason.*

Burke regarded as folly the Enlightenment program of willed, abstractly written reform. Such a program not only violated the manifold and ever-present contingency of human nature; it also violated the very character of history, the almost biological unfolding of those institutions of social being that are designated by the "great blossomers," the deep-rooted sources of the natural order.

Burke distinguished between the English Revolution of 1688 and the French Revolution of 1789, both of which certain political parties and radicals in Britain tended to confound by association. In Burke's interpretation, the principles of the English Revolution were *sacredly* spelled out in a series of unalterable documents, ranging from the Magna Carta to the great tradition of English legal practice. The British constitution, although never in a written form like that of the U.S. constitution, was "natural"; it embodied the organic actions of English history. Its fundamental principles had been written into various documents, which constitute a corporate contract for the English people. These documents, Burke reasoned, form a series of historical and legal precedents, as if they were a single coherent document.

Burke insisted that the British constitution forms a concrete link with the real world of law and justice; hence, with the lived experience of the English people. He contrasted these "human" documents with the various proclamations that (he claimed) have no coherent link with the historical and lived experience of the French people. The French revolutionaries "act like the comedians at a fair . . . amidst the tumultuous cries of a mixed mob of ferocious men" and of "women lost to shame." Burke stressed the "insolent fancies" that "direct, control . . . and domineer . . . with a strange mixture of servile petulance and proud, presumptuous authority." [22] Authority is for Burke the heart of the matter, even as it was in his earlier epistolary attack on Paine's style and method as empty of valid content because they were mere surface constructions not founded on the bedrock of substantive historical knowledge.

Burke's famous lament for the death of chivalry is as much about the death of the old order as it is about the degradation and death of kings and queens. When the "decent drapery of life" is "rudely torn off," a king is reduced to "but a man, a queen is but a woman; a woman is but an animal,—and an animal not of the highest order." Burke then conjures up the "plight" of the French queen; he describes Marie Antoinette fleeing *en déshabillé* from her frenzied pursuers—a queen who barely touched "this orb" but drifted above the horizon "glittering like the morning-star, full of life and splendour and joy." It was hardly an argument, as Paine would point out, but it was, nonetheless, an integral part of Burke's political position. [23]

The central metaphor Burke used for this new corrupting and degrading power was derived from the account of the Tower of Babel in the first book of Scripture—not surprising, given Burke's unquestioned association of religion and politics throughout his book. Characteristically, Burke assailed those who (like Paine, we may surmise from Burke's epistolary attack) employ a "language" that is "in the *patois* of fraud, in the cant and gibberish of hypocrisy." As "fallen" illiterate speech, such degenerative intellectual dialect must for Burke inevitably yield a world of madness where humanity is obliged to adopt all the crude and corrupt measures suggested by clubs "composed of a monstrous motley of all conditions, rogues, and nations." [24] Language is an important issue for Burke, a language properly validated by the social order (political and religious) established, as if by divine sanction, over the ages of human experience.

For all his dark pessimism, Burke situates his countermessage in *Reflections* in a reaffirmation of the power of properly warranted language. Without an inkling of concern that his own language might evidence the same problem of authenticity he attributes to the *patois* of his opposition, without an inkling that the social order he valorizes might be licensed by mere language rather than vice versa, Burke affirms the ability of the English people to recognize the deceptiveness of a new language of Babel. This audience would be assisted presumably by Burke's own words, which his British audience presumably would recognize as credited by the same *political and religious* forces informing the British constitution. Then this audience would properly dissociate the radicals and revolutionists from solid, sound-minded Englishmen, like Burke.[25] "We know that *we* have made no discoveries, and we think that no new discoveries are to be made, in morality,—nor many in the great principles of government, nor in the ideas of liberty, which were understood before we were born."[26] Within half a century Burke's analysis behind his somber clairvoyance would take on formidable weight in the history of France.

Dramatic Performance: Paine's *Rights of Man*

On learning of the imminent publication of Burke's work, Paine left France and arrived in London on 7 March 1791. On 13 March the first part of *Rights of Man; or, Analytical Strictures in the Constitution of Great Britain and Ireland* appeared in the bookstalls. It sold out within a few hours. A second and a third edition were published by the end of March, a fourth on 18 April, a fifth on 4 May, and a sixth on 28 May. Each edition sold for three shillings, two less than Burke's book. Whereas Paine estimated the sale of *Rights* throughout Britain to have extended to "not less than between forty and fifty thousand" (1:350), a recent estimate suggests two hundred thousand copies were sold in England by 1792.[27]

Paine's pamphlet came under immediate summary condemnation and was swiftly banned. To own or sell a copy was a criminal offense. By that time, the summer of 1792, Paine had left England again and had become an active member in the French Revolution with a seat in the National Convention. In February 1792, he returned to England to publish part 2 of *Rights*, but once more fled to France to avoid a trial on the charge of seditious libel provoked by his book.

Paine's trial, held in the London Guildhall on 18 December 1792, attracted considerable attention. Paine was accused of "a deliberate intention to vilify and degrade . . . the whole constitution of government of the country," and to represent "the regal part of the government . . . as an oppressive and abominable tyranny."[28] In partial response, Sir Thomas Erskine (1750–1823), who conducted Paine's defense, tried to show that the issue was not libel but the right of every freeborn Englishman to liberty of speech in general and liberty of the press in particular.[29] One contemporary spoke of this trial as "the most extraordinary prosecution that has been commenced in this country";[30] nevertheless, after the judge's summation of the arguments, the jury found Paine guilty without even retiring to consider its verdict. *Rights of Man* was a banned book.

Whatever this verdict might suggest and whatever the nature of the argument of principle in the two books, the encounter between Burke and Paine was also personal. Whether or not the relationship between Burke and Paine was as uneasy as we suspect, it is certain that for obscure reasons Paine pursued Burke's attention and in various subtle ways deferred to Burke's "superior" social position; it was Paine who had sought out the association from the first, had reestablished it after Burke ended it, and had even submitted his French correspondence to Burke's validating perusal. In light of these details, one might surmise Paine's sense of humiliation and eventual outrage on reading his associate's wounding quotations from Paine's own letters. It was as if Burke, apparently a father figure in some sense to Paine, had suddenly taken advantage of his younger associate's vulnerability in their relationship.

And can we doubt that Burke's *Appeal from the New to the Old Whigs,* published on 3 August 1791 in response to part 3 of *Rights of Man,* only angered Paine more? In this work Burke quoted a number of passages from *Rights of Man,* without once identifying the author, and then dismissed Paine's points at issue as mere "Whig principles" not worthy of an "attempt in the smallest degree to refute them."[31] Burke had assumed a position of established, unquestioned authority, dismissing

Paine as someone inferior, someone of lower intelligence and class, someone beneath the honor of being named.[32] That Paine perceived the insult clearly is suggested in his retort, "I see nothing in Mr. Burke's 'Appeal' worth taking much notice of," and in his justification for not having responded so far to attacks on the first part of *Rights of Man:* "I believe that a man may write himself out of reputation when nobody else can do it" (1:349–50). Subtly Paine had returned Burke's insult and had also asserted that his already established reputation constitutes his authority.

Paine was motivated, then, by references in *Reflections* to some of his most personal beliefs expressed in the January 1790 letter to Burke concerning the likely spread of the French Revolution across Europe as well as by his opposition to Burke's views, particularly to Burke's allusion to "that grand magazine of offensive weapons, the rights of man."[33] The scurrility on "rights of man" gave Paine the title of his first reply, although of course the phrase was available to him as well in the French "Declaration of the Rights of Man and Citizens" adopted by the National Assembly on 29 August 1789 and included in its entirety in Paine's book.

This "Declaration" reads in part as follows: "*Men are born, and always continue free, and equal in respect to their rights. Civil distinctions, therefore, can be founded only on public utility*" (1:314). The idea of the natural or essential equality of mankind had been articulated elsewhere, in Jefferson's preamble to the Declaration of Independence, for instance. Paine's translation of the statement found in the French Declaration was new insofar as it suggested that all social inequalities should be rationally defensible. This idea seems innocent enough, but taken seriously it is a notion profoundly subversive to established authority figures, including Burke.

While essaying to answer and counter Burke's main arguments and reasons, Paine sought to set forth his own principles of society, not only as they are founded on the rule of law, but also as they may be seen to lead to a condition of mankind suitable to the new time he believed was now dawning. He did not, however, take up Burke's central principle that societies and governments should rely on the precedents of the past, which they should be very reluctant to change. Rather, Paine had his own two points of attack, one narrow and limited, the other broad and anticipatory of his *Age of Reason*.[34]

The first, the simpler and narrower one, was Paine's consideration that the French Revolution was aimed at overthrowing the power of a money-hungry aristocracy seeking to perpetuate the system of paper currency and public credit on which its power rested. On this point Paine was able to exercise considerable talent and ingenuity in determining ways that numbers, statistics, the elements of numerical order and probability, and the telltale signs of social order are reflected in money. The way of numbers, we note in passing, would inform one of Paine's chief inquiries into Scripture in *The Age of Reason.*

Paine arrayed gatherings of taxes, expenditures, debts, and financial matters in tables (1:432–43) which, no doubt, most modern readers skip as having only immediate, contemporary argument and interest. Yet they were one of Paine's key points in refuting some of Burke's central contentions, namely, that a people's way of life is best maintained by continuing the well-tried and proved governmental practices of the past. For Paine, the Revolution had been, in a sense, a national and democratic takeover of the debts of the French crown. Paine argued that revolutionaries must seize the credit of the state because they now live in a world transformed by credit. The state must assume power over the lives of its citizens by making certain that their fiduciary status is maintained to their security and livelihood, in contrast to the traditional aristocratic financial system subject to the whims of some political party, the manipulations of greedy landholders, and the exigencies of peace or war. [35]

Paine's second point of attack was informed by a rather simple ideal: a republic of a purposeful body of citizens joined in a common culture seen as an extension and manifestation of republican feeling and thinking. There would be a dual republic formed as one. The first would be a republic of belief, a new and inevitably forthcoming body of citizen-believers in a modern state now emerging through the practical regeneration of nature, humanity, and society. This republic of belief would be based on the realization of "natural rights," on which their civil rights would be based, and the reliance upon the truths of reason to dispel ignorance and superstition, presently the twin flaws of human nature.

In imagining this republic of belief, Paine anticipates *The Age of Reason* when he necessarily touches on the issues of religion. In *Rights of Man* Paine envisions an advanced, truly devout body of believers who recognize one God through the disclosures of science and who, consequently, reject formal religions, including their clergy and governmental lackeys. This republic of belief, of "natural rights," would also include a second component, nonbelievers such as skeptics and atheists who are unable to accept the general faith of the new religious body; these nonbelievers, however, must conform with the majority in observing certain common rules and laws.

Paine had been especially piqued by Burke's insistent charge of atheism, and his notion of a republic of *belief* was meant, in part, as an answer. Despite his criticism of Reverend Price's manner, Burke had likewise comfortably mingled religion and politics, as typified, for instance, when he noted in the *Appeal,* "It is now obvious to the world, that a theory concerning government may become as much a cause of fanaticism as a dogma in religion. There is a boundary to men's passions, when they act from feeling; none when they are under the influence of imagination."[36]

In response to Burke's method, Paine specifically and pointedly complains that "one of the continual choruses of Mr. Burke's book, is 'church and state'" (1:292). He indicts Burke for constructing a "political church," not only by simplistically associating government and religion, but also by mimicking in his political views, "as of divine authority," the tyranny of magisterial papacy: "He has shortened his journey to Rome, by appealing to the power of this infallible Parliament of former days" (1:252–53). Looking forward to *The Age of Reason,* moreover, Paine notes in passing that rhetorical strategies such as Burke's had already been denounced by a French thinker, Voltaire (François Marie Arouet, 1694–1778), whose "forte lay in exposing and ridiculing the superstitions which priestcraft, united with statecraft, had interwoven with governments" (1:299).

As we saw in *Common Sense* and the *Crisis* papers, Paine sought (without sensing the contradiction in his manner) an ostensible justification for his voice by relying on Scripture. In the first part of *Rights of Man,* in contrast, Scripture is hardly present. Once Paine alludes by analogy to the biblical version of the Creation (1:274). He subsequently cites St. Paul (1 Cor. 13:11) in a manner designed specifically not to invoke the Bible as a legitimation of his comments: "A certain writer, of some antiquity, says, 'When I was a child, I thought as a child: but when I became a man, I put away childish things'" (1:286). In the second part of *Rights of Man* Paine makes no overt references to Scripture.

In his confrontation with Burke, Paine not only was losing an authority figure of some apparent personal value to him, but also was losing the very scriptural authority on which his first works depended. For finally in response to Burke's seeming betrayal of him, Paine would do more than depose Burke's pontifications. Shortly, he would in *The Age of Reason* depose the supremacy of religion itself as the main prop behind Burke's assumed stance and voice of superiority, both founded only on the "assumed authority of the dead" (1:252). In *Rights of Man* he would emphasize briefly how the association of religion and government corrupted the church (1:292), whereas in the later book he would stress how the association corrupted the state. In Paine's opinion, "Religion is very improperly made a political machine" (1:451), and this machinery of the "church and state," the "political church," comprises "a succession of barriers, or a sort of turnpike gates," through which humanity must pass, an "artificial chasm" putting humanity at "a vast distance from [its] Maker" (1:275).

It is unlikely that Paine knew Burke's private religious beliefs and convictions. But he could strike at a generalized, a gentleman's, religion by firmly equating the Christian church with chicanery, corruption, and civic oppression. There, Paine must have thought, Burke would have no answer, or at least not any answer that would escape ridicule; Paine doubtless thought Burke would never descend to be made to appear ridiculous. In assailing Christianity and its biblical ground, Paine would damage the argumentative strategy of his own early work, but he did not stop to consider that problem. Those works were in the past, and for him the past was always "dead" in relation to the living present moment. The new nation had been formed and could not be lost by any such reassessment of his now dead arguments.

In the final pages of *Rights of Man* Paine sets forth "in what light religion appears to [him]." Paine's religion, as "acceptable in [the Deity's] sight and being the best service [one] can perform," would "conciliate mankind" and would "extirpate the horrid practise of war and break the chains of slavery and oppression" (1:452). Contrasted to the sharpness of rhetoric characterizing Paine's attack on Burke earlier in the book, Paine's epilogue appears mild indeed, possibly suggesting an almost religious sense of appeasement and charity. Here, in some underlying sense, Paine seems wistful, as if still a little reluctant on a personal level to break with Burke permanently.

On the surface, however, this change in tone may also indicate Paine's belief that he has made his case and can come to rest with the descent of a curtain, as it were, after having presented an irrefutable argument against a now presumably fallen adversary. The epilogue possibly intimates a sense of achieved self-crediting to some extent, so that the speaker, a person of evident "reputation" (as he himself told his readers), can now afford a different tack, a modified voice. But that voice, nonetheless, never becomes emancipated from its confrontation with established authority. In *Rights of Man* Burke plays the part played by King George III in *Common Sense* and the *Crisis* papers[37]—the authority figure, the father figure, deposed. And in combating these representatives of an aristocracy originating in "governments founded upon conquest" (1:288), Paine replicates in his performance a similar attempt to prevail over, to subjugate, his rival.

In *Rights of Man* Paine refers to Burke's "paradoxical genius" (1:250): "It is in his paradoxes that we must look for his arguments"

(1:258). Pertinently, Paine's own voice in *Rights of Man* originates in paradox; for it always remains respondent to and directed at the monarch-like figure of Burke as the very ground of its own being. Paine's voice here necessarily depends on and identifies with the authority it deposes. Its very opposition, which is its motivation, serves as the underlying "polar truth or principle" by which Paine "attempts to steer his course" (1:318). In this sense, Carl B. Cone's succinct observation, "without Burke, no Tom Paine,"[38] is indeed apt.

In *Rights of Man* Paine's voice asserts that its warrant derives from "natural rights," which claim appropriates Burke's manner, a manner Paine described "as of divine authority." Paine's appeal to natural rights displaces justification from the self (wounded by Burke) and ascribes it to the divinely dictated laws of nature. Pertinently, Paine also approaches his task indirectly, as if obscuring its origin in his wounded self, the immediate personal cause of his undertaking: "I promised some of the friends of the Revolution . . . that whenever Mr. Burke's pamphlet came forth, I would answer it" (1:245). Was he asked, or did he volunteer? The origin of the book—Paine's voice—remains uncertain in its explanation of its prime mover.

These deflections aside, the theatricality of Paine's voice forcefully derives from and aims at—that is, it fundamentally always identifies itself in relation to—the authority it deposes, the established, paternal, aristocratic, regal voice represented by Burke. Despite Paine's strategy of claiming a polar opposition to Burke, the execution of this very maneuver blurs the border between his own and his adversary's sovereignty of voice. Moreover, if Paine's assault were indeed to prevail, where henceforth would the need (the cause) for his voice preside? Paine's pronouncements are fundamentally situated on the very Burkean texts it refutes. And one might wonder, Does the tapering off of force at the end of *Rights of Man* hint at a trace of anxiety in the assault on Burke, that father figure of sorts to whom the now rebellious son oddly once deferred; does it, in other words, hint at the necessary diminishment of Paine's own voice as it attempts to outperform, to outmimic, and to overpower Burke's voice, the unacknowledged source (origin, cause) of Paine's oracular pronouncements in *Rights of Man?*

Curiously, that an oracular voice is merely a theatrical production, a role or fiction without any empirically based justification, is suggested by both Burke and Paine. Burke, as we noted, designated Paine's epistolary comments as a "*patois* of fraud," as "cant," as "gibberish"; and he designated Paine and the French revolutionaries as "comedians at a fair," ridiculous participants in a "monstrous tragic-comic scene." In *Reflections* Burke not only attacked the corrupt Babel-like language of the revolutionaries, but also he utilized allusions to the stage as a *reductio ad absurdum* to undermine the empirical ground, the soundness, of his opposition, whose argumentation in this depraved language is as fictional as speech in a stage drama.[39]

Paine reverses the charge, accusing Burke of using virtually every "epithet of abuse to be found in the English language," and asks if this is "the language of a rational man" (1:249, 258). Moreover, just prior to recalling Burke's imaginative depiction of the "plight" of Marie Antoinette fleeing *en déshabillé* from her frenzied pursuers, Paine alludes to the stage as if parodying Burke:

> As to the tragic paintings by which Mr. Burke has outraged his own imagination, and seeks to work upon that of his readers, they are very well calculated for theatrical representation, where facts are manufactured for the sake of show, and accommodated to produce, through the weakness of sympathy, a weeping effect. But Mr. Burke should recollect that he is writing history, and not *plays;* and that his readers will expect truth, and not the spouting rant of high-toned declamation. (1:258–59)

The italicizing of the word *plays* seems particularly pointed in Paine's refunding of the accusation that mere imaginative fiction informs the speech of his former acquaintance. And consider a related comment by Paine:

> I cannot consider Mr. Burke's book in scarcely any other light than a dramatic performance; and he must, I think, have considered it in the same light himself, by the poetic liberties he has taken of omitting some facts, distorting others, and making the machinery bend to produce a stage effect. (1:267–68)

The phrases *theatrical representation* and *dramatic performance* go to the heart of the matter. Authority, as we noted in our Introduction, depends on the person interpreting deeds and voice as signs; authority, in the most extreme sense of this signification, ultimately remains only an imaginative performance declaring self-authorship. But that detail escaped both Burke and Paine, not only concerning the imperious pronouncements each made against the other, but also concerning the social structures each advocated in opposition to the other.

If Paine could not see how his response to Edmund Burke comprised one more instance of the antiquarian formula of "authority against author-ity" (1:273), he apparently also did not notice his own reenactment of his opponent's manner in the commentary situated precisely between his two extended attacks on Burke's "theatrical exaggerations" (1:267). Just as he speaks of the "scene of Mr. Burke's drama" (1:272), he refers to his own depiction of the taking of the Bastille as a "tremendous scene" (1:261), which he then unfolds in much detail, including background images of stone piles, narrow streets, and multistoried houses (1:263). Paine reports that "all the playhouses and places of entertainment . . . were shut up" in observance of the monumental drama of Bastille Day (1:263), and the theatrical performance of his voice in *Rights of Man* narrating that drama of historical truth intends to shut down *Reflections on the French Revolu-tion,* a Babel-like artifice of spouted "rant of high-toned declamation."

Its specific grounding in Burke notwithstanding, *Rights of Man* was but an instance, albeit a significant one, in a long argument that included and went beyond politics, the French Revolution, and human rights. The debate ventured into the domain of religion, as we have seen; for it was in and about religion all the time. Although there might not usually be direct or tangible connections made between political and religious ideas and argument, there could be—and there were—definite combinations of political and religious ideas all through that decade. So when Paine fixed on one, he was as well delving into the other, as moments in *Rights of Man* indicate. When Paine focused on Burke's association with religious authority and his mingling of it with political legitimacy in *Rights of Man,* the issue of religion came logically out of the issue of politics because the connection was already a feature of Paine's intellectual milieu, as was also evident in Reverend Price's work. The response to Burke in *Rights of Man,* then, initiated Paine's keener perception of this connection in his thought; and aptly providing a transition to *The Age of Reason, Rights of Man* concludes with Paine's admonition concerning the ways whereby "religion is very improperly made a political machine" (1:451).

As *The Age of Reason* documents, Paine's protest against social ills and political evils would become virtually the same protest against Scrip-ture. Whereas in *Common Sense* and the *Crisis* papers Paine had problem-atically relied directly on Scripture for license to depose King George III, he only rarely and briefly alluded to Scripture in *Rights of Man.* Neverthe-less, just as he reenacted (while opposing) a sense of monarchical divine right in his earlier publications, he equally problematically confiscated the Burkean imperious manner, "as of divine authority" (1:253), in the later book. In both instances Paine tried to outperform his doctrinaire rivals; but because his voice was always defined against and aimed at theirs, originated from and depended on theirs, he finally mimicked them. As we will see, Paine's maneuvers to legitimate his pronouncements would become especially enigmatic in *The Age of Reason,* which would challenge the dominion of Scripture itself.

3

The Context of Paine's
Biblical Learning

In the final decade of the eighteenth century a tradition, a canon, of biblical scholarship dating from the Protestant Reformation was undergoing major change. This change would need a longer time to manifest itself fully, but its most important signs and exponents were recognizably present. What may be called "enmity" bound together a culture, a body of belief, grown so complex that its contradictions could no longer be reconciled.

If in the sixteenth and seventeenth centuries skepticism was contained by orthodoxy, by the end of the eighteenth century, when skepticism had itself come to power, orthodoxy would assume the role of contender and advocate. In trying to maintain continuity and authority, Christian culture, primarily Protestant, had depended on an attitude toward history as divine providence and toward Scripture as divine revelation that the skeptics and freethinkers of England and France called into question. What if the Old Testament version of the origin of the world seemed to be incompatible with the history of the world as experienced or with the way atoms moved according to Isaac Newton's laws of motion? And what if the Bible were an anthology, and the Christian part had been added at a late date? The skeptics and freethinkers reopened settled questions in which buried contradictions had always lodged.

The history of biblical learning, like the history of modern culture, is a network of discrepancies. For some time, in fact, English and Continental thinkers had reasoned that Moses did not write the Pentateuch, except the laws of Deuteronomy, which were specifically attributed to him; that the authorship and chronology of composition of the rest of the Old Testament were far later in time than traditionally maintained; and that the basic organization of the Old Testament was the work of scribes, including the scribe Ezra, following the return of the Jews from the Babylonian Captivity. Indeed, scholars of various schools and professions, as we will note, proposed that diverse hands in the past had been busy manipulating the form and even the wording of the sacred text; therefore, they reasoned that a modern reading of Scripture ought to be devised within a contemporary rather than an outmoded point of view. Orthodox believers and skeptics, religionists and freethinkers, *pompiers* and avant-garde composed a ceaseless opposition on the question of scriptural verity.

In the decade when Paine wrote *The Age of Reason,* this debate was already well under way, especially in France. Its lines and directions were being charted, its speculative outline was already in place, through the partial criticism and innuendo of such authors as Isaac LaPeyrere, Richard Simon, Pierre Bayle, Anthony Shaftesbury, David Hume, Voltaire, Henry St. John Bolingbroke, Nicolas-Antoine Boulanger, Denis Diderot, and Baron d'Holbach.[1] Moreover, the great mass of supporting evidence, used later particularly by certain early nineteenth-century German scholars, was already tentatively presented in summary form in magazine articles and reviews that were, as we will see, readily available to Paine and his contemporaries.

Consider, for instance, several observations in a letter (10 August 1787) that Thomas Jefferson sent from Paris (that hotbed of radical fomentation) to Peter Carr. Jefferson candidly instructs Carr to "read the Bible . . . as you would read Livy or Tacitus. The facts which are within the ordinary course of nature, you will believe on the authority of the writer, as you do those of the same kind in Livy and Tacitus." Jefferson then details, as an example of scriptural unreliability, the problems associated with the biblical report that the sun stood still for several hours. He cautions Carr against accepting this improbability or any similar one presented in the account of Jesus in the New Testament merely because of "the pretensions of the writer to inspiration from God"; on the contrary, Carr should be guided by his "own reason," the "only oracle given [him] by heaven." Jefferson firmly concludes that if such skepticism "ends in a belief that there is no God, you will find incitements to virtue in the comfort and pleasantness you feel in its exercise, and the love of others it will procure you."[2] Jefferson's open-mindedness about Scripture and Christian beliefs based on it did not remain private, and in time his political adversaries tarred and feathered him with several ready contumelious epithets.

William Godwin's *Caleb Williams* (1794), which appeared in the same year as the English edition of the first part of Paine's *Age of Reason,* was subjected to similar abuse; for it argued the "truth" that "the spirit and character of the government" in contemporary England were under a rule fixed by the age-old and evil alliance of church and state.[3] In that same year Mary Wollstonecraft, Godwin's wife, published *Historical and Moral View of the Origin and Progress of the French Revolution; and the Effect It Has Produced in Europe,* a book that touched on some of the central principles treated in Paine's inquiry. "The Revolution in France exhibits," she declared, "the contrast . . . between the narrow opinions of superstition, and the enlightened sentiments of masculine and improved philosophy." Her sense of "masculine" philosophy remains unclear, but certain is her attribution of the "barbaric" situation in France before the Revolution to those two key powers Paine would affirm as the very enemies of enlightenment and freedom: "superstition and despotism, hand in hand." She speaks of the "oppressive tyranny . . . of priests[, who] have erected their tremendous structures of imposition," as well as the entrenched powerful "privileged classes, which had their origin in barbarous folly."[4] The attacked "priests" were not silent, and in their war against what they called *atheism* they addressed themselves to setting forth the inevitable power of divine judgment in the affairs of men and government. A prominent expression for their side at the time was, "Religion [is] a Preservative Against Barbarism and Anarchy."[5]

Preceding Biblical Commentary

As Paine admitted, he did not have a Bible in hand when he wrote the first part of *The Age of Reason,* a fact testifying to the extensiveness of his familiarity with Scripture. He did, however, have a copy of the Bible when he penned the second part in 1795. The translation he used was an eighteenth-century printing of the King James (or Authorized) Version of 1611. Although the particular edition cannot be identified—Paine had no need to specify it, since for him all Bibles were unquestionably the same text—something needs to be said about the form and printing of his copy to determine what Paine would make of it in his analysis and judgment.[6]

Every copy of the Scriptures printed in the later eighteenth century, as in the century preceding, was in double column. Every verse was numbered for ready reference and citation; and each page had at the top a summary statement of the subject or content of that page. Furthermore, there were small-print, italicized cross-references in the margins keyed to verses or passages elsewhere in Scripture, references linking persons, events, and significant themes across the whole range of Scripture from Genesis to Revelation. These citations were of great use to ministers and ordinary readers who wished to trace out (sometimes typologically) the intricate "leadings" or associations of event to outcome, of early thought to its later resolution, and of prophecy to fulfillment throughout all Scripture. The other aid to readers was a chronology appearing as dates at the top of each column and in the margins. This dating assigned 4004 B.C. to Creation in Genesis and moved to the birth of the Messiah in the year 1 at the end of that term. Paine, who called these dates "the Bible Chronology" devised by "chronologists," reported that "there is a series of chronology printed in the margin of every page, for the purpose of showing how long the historical matters stated in each page happened, or are supposed to have happened, before Christ, and, consequently, the distance of time between one historical circumstance and another" (1:524–25).

Paine was probably not aware that this dating was the work of Archbishop James Ussher, primate of Armaugh and of Ireland, who presented this ancient chronology in *Annales Veteris Testimenti* (1650–54), better known in its English translation as *The Annals of the World Deduced from the Origin of Time, and Continued to the Beginning of the Emperour Vespasians Reign* (1658). By dating the Creation as occurring in October 4004 B.C. and by arranging the whole of Scripture from this point, Ussher had accommodated both biblical and all known ancient pagan histories and calendars to the grand design that divine providence seemed to have instituted for the world.

Ussher's chronology, which still appears in many editions of the Bible today, was regarded in the eighteenth century as so manifestly, even divinely, true to every event in Scripture that it seemed to have been virtually revealed by the Deity, that is to say, put in the text by God himself. Pertinently, an edition printed in 1702 placed Ussher's dates in the very body of Scripture. Thereafter his chronology always appeared at the top of a column or in the margins of the pages. So like the copy of Scripture that Paine read in his younger years, the one he relied on after his release from prison and throughout the writing of the second part of *The Age of Reason* fixed all biblical events precisely according to the year, sometimes even the month and day, along the divine span of time designated by Ussher and then identified with the biblical text itself.

Because Paine had no knowledge of Hebrew, he could not read the Old Testament in the original. Without Greek he could not read the Septuagint, the version of the Old Testament translated into Greek by Hebrew scholars in Alexandria several centuries before Christ. Nor could he read the New Testament in its original Greek version. He made no mention of or apology for this deficiency, nor did he need to do so, in his opinion. He claimed to be an intelligent reader who could rely on "reason and philosophy" alone to approach the Bible on "its own ground," so that "historically and chronologically" Scripture itself would "prove" just what it truly conveys and means (1:467, 524).

Paine's declaration of freedom from any authority other than his own mind—reason and philosophy—is as suspect as are his rhetorical strategies in deposing King George III in *Common Sense* and the regal minion Burke in *Rights of Man*. In fact, as we indicate in this chapter, Paine's French, English, and American milieu, whatever the distinctions of its various cultures in other regards, shared a complex, if conflicted, body of commentary on the issues he would treat in *The Age of Reason*.[7] Paine came to the writing of this book with considerable knowledge, however gained, of advanced, liberal biblical thought. In spite of Paine's general erasure of the details of this influence on him, we can recover features of the thought of persons that significantly informed his international intellectual milieu and that, in turn, seem to have had (in one or another form) a bearing on his own understanding of Scripture.[8]

Paine opens a door to this inquiry and, incidentally, raises the reader's skepticism concerning his claim to the complete independence of his investigation by actually alluding in his book to a few commentators on Scripture. Two are particularly important: Baruch Spinoza and "Fauste" (1:547, 586).

"Fauste" is Faustus of Milevus, a late-fourth-century Manichean propagandist who, as Paine notes, had won fame as a rhetorician in Rome. When Faustus visited Carthage in 383—Paine says it was "about the year 400" (1:586)—Augustine, himself a Manichee, took direction from him, but eventually found Faustus to be a fraud. Faustus's teachings have not survived, although they can be partly reconstructed from Augustine's *Contra Faustum Manichaeum* (c. 400). As a minor, although legendary person, he apparently appealed to Paine as an exponent of an anti-Christian, antibiblical point of view; for "Fauste" was credited with having taken the phrase "the Gospel according to" to imply that the Four Gospels were made up from some later account rather than from the original versions.

Spinoza (1632–77) similarly must have appealed to Paine as the philosopher who first challenged the traditional belief that Moses composed the Pentateuch. In *Tractatus Theologico-politicus* (1670), later translated into English as *A Treatise Partly Theological, and Partly Political* (1689), Spinoza attacked the notion of Mosaic authorship. Paine cited from a French translation of *Tractatus* (1678) because an English translation of Spinoza's book, even the one published in 1737, was probably unavailable to him in Paris.

Spinoza anticipated Paine on a number of points concerning biblical interpretation. First, he found abundant evidence suggesting that the author of the Pentateuch lived long after the time of Moses. His candidate for this role was Ezra, who assembled the Pentateuch and the historical accounts following it "by cutting and shuffling" the accounts of various writers, sometimes setting them down as they actually appeared and sometimes introducing later, anachronistic narratives that had no place in the original record. For Spinoza, the text of the Old Testament was a kind of jumble, filled with repetitions, inconsistencies, and historical improbabilities. [9]

Like "Abenezra" (Abraham ben Meir Ibn Ezra [1098–1164]), mentioned in *The Age of Reason* (1:547) and celebrated later in Robert Browning's "Rabbi Ben Ezra"), Spinoza also anticipated Paine's attribution of the book of Job to "a Gentile" who wrote in a different language from Hebrew. This work must have been "translated out of another language," Spinoza reported, "because it seems to affect the Heathen Poesy." Moreover, Spinoza observed, the author of certain parts of the Old Testament did not "call things and places by those very names which they had at the time of which the Writer speaketh, but by the names which they were known by, in the Writer['s] own time." The original names of persons and places had been lost or misread, and, therefore, "any rule or any reason to be observed in expounding Scripture" granted "every Man [the] phancy to forge what he pleases."

In disparaging words similar to Paine's observations on the same subject (1:547–48), Spinoza wrote:

> If anyone pays attention to the way in which all the histories and precepts . . . are set down promiscuously and without order, with no regard for dates; and further, how the same story is often repeated, sometimes in a different version, he will easily, I say, discern that all the materials were promiscuously collected and heaped together, in order that they might at some subsequent time be more readily examined and reduced to order. Not only these five books, but also the narratives contained in the remaining seven, going down to the destruction of the city [Jerusalem], are compiled in the same way. [10]

When the history of Israel was written by scribes such as Ezra, Spinoza maintained, there was imposed on an earlier time the historical perspective of the age of the later writers and compilers. Thus, the whole of the Old Testament history was made to accommodate the exigencies of the Jews after the return from the Babylonian Captivity. By so construing the biblical narratives, Spinoza called attention to the frequent repetitions in various stories and passages, and to numerous contradictions between various texts. It is in light of these observations, among others, that Spinoza has become recognized as one of the founders of modern historical criticism of the Bible.

Faustus, Ibn Ezra, and Spinoza are three biblical authorities Paine cited in his text; another name, as we will observe shortly, appears in footnotes to his commentary on the New Testament. Paine merely mentions Faustus, Ibn Ezra, and Spinoza, and gives no overt sign of having derived from them issues and concerns manifest overtly in his book. Paine mentions them in this manner because they stated, and stated well, principles that were pervasive in late-eighteenth-century comments on and charges against the Bible. In this sense they were part of all manner of discussion in Paine's time. Nevertheless, whatever Paine's final motivation for citing them, these allusions intimate his need for some outside authority that subverts his claim to no ground other than the reasoning of his own independent (self-authorizing) mind against the corrupt biblical text. His indebtedness to others was, in fact, larger than these three seemingly casual references might suggest; for, as Jefferson's earlier letter indicates, Paine lived in—and he had to be fully aware of living in—a climate of revisionary thinking about Scripture.

The major issue of the authenticity of Scripture was, moreover, an old and contentious one, dating back to the early Christians and continuing through the debates and controversies of the Reformation to the late eighteenth century. By the late eighteenth century a formidable skepticism on this subject had reached an apogee of sorts in the writings of such questioners as John Toland, Jeremiah Jones, and Anthony Collins, all of whom were influenced by John Locke's empiricism.

John Toland (1670–1722) was an Irish Roman Catholic who converted to Protestantism and published *Christianity not Mysterious* (1696). He argued, in anticipation of Paine's position later, that reason alone could be used to assess the question of the inspiration of Scripture. His own application of the methods of reason resulted in an attack on the "ridiculous or arrogant Pretenders," who maintained the sanctity of Scripture only because of their love of personal power and financial gain.[11] In his *Life of Milton* (1698), Toland renewed his charge by insinuating in a single contentious passage that many of the writings of early Christianity, including presumably the New Testament, were not authentic but had been contrived by later apologists. In *Amyntor; or, A Defence of Milton's Life* (1699), Toland more specifically affirmed that not a single book of the New Testament was properly attributed to the apostles—that each book was actually forged by their adversaries. Toland's innuendoes and arguments caused a scandal in their time—*Christianity not Mysteri-*

ous was burned in Ireland—and they drew forth a wide assortment of angry replies from various defenders of the Christian faith.

The sanctity of the Bible was assailed as well by Jeremiah Jones (1693–1724), a Nonconformist minister. In *New and Full Method of Settling the Canonical Authority of the New Testament* (1726, 1727), an edition that also appeared at the end of the eighteenth century, Jones conducted a detailed historical and philological examination "to determine the canonical authority of any book, or books" by "finding out the testimony or traditions of those who lived nearest the time in which the books were written."[12] Equally telling was *A Discourse of the Grounds and Reasons of the Christian Religion* (1724), in which Anthony Collins (1676–1729) sought to undermine arguments for the unity of the two Testaments. The Old Testament prophecies cited in the Old Testament as proofs that Jesus was the Messiah, Collins argued, are not literal predictions of Jesus at all, "not Proofs according to Scholastick Rules."[13] Collins reduced prophetic foretelling to mere facts that could be historically pinpointed (if they were true at all) in the manner of an almanac with dates corroborated to the particular times and seasons. If, Collins reasoned, the Bible is the supreme moral teaching that its proponents affirm, then it surely reflects the lowest standard of behavior representative, it would seem, of a barbarous age. Collins's arguments elicited considerable response from clergymen, and one of his later works was even satirized by Jonathan Swift.

A number of English divines throughout the eighteenth century further called the Scriptures into question, among them Symon Patrick, Humphrey Prideaux, and Samuel Clarke. Matthew Tindal (c.1655–1733), some of whose writings were either proscribed or condemned, excited attention by raising a formidable array of questions that Christians had evaded concerning Adam and Eve's first sin of concupiscence, Rahab the harlot, the sacrifice of Isaac and Jephthah's daughter, patriarchal lying, the slaughter of women and children, and the destruction of whole cities. Another impressive inquiry was penned by Nathaniel Lardner (1684–1768), whose *The Credibility of Gospel History* (1727–57) applied immense learning and alarming candor in reconciling the discrepancies in the New Testament. By exposing these discrepancies while trying to account for them, Lardner provided a mine of information for those skeptics who were raising questions concerning the authenticity of Scripture and the validity of Christianity as founded on the Bible.

Certain eighteenth-century inquirers perceived that a varying structure or deposit of fragments and discontinuous pieces lay behind the appearance of biblical wholeness and uniformity. This fragmentation, even apparent confusion, had resulted, they surmised, from a long, discontinuous historical process. In their opinion, to penetrate into this disarray was insufficient; it was necessary to trace the temporal human factor (history) in the process by which these varying parts had been assembled into the form that they have assumed over the centuries.

This concern with detecting the human factor included the New Testament. One of the most cogent commentaries on the gospel miracles, for instance, appeared in Conyers Middleton's *Free Inquiry into the Miraculous Powers* (1749). Although Paine specifically reported, in 1802, that he had "lately met with the writings of Doctor Conyers Middleton" (2:882), the similarities between their arguments and even expressions in *The Age of Reason,* as chapter 4 will indicate, raise the question of whether or not Paine was in some way familiar with Middleton's thought much earlier.

Middleton repudiates the well-established position of the defenders of orthodoxy that miracles are a crucial feature of Christian belief because they herald the divine nature of Jesus' revelation. Like David Hume, Middleton claims that miracles are not extraordinary or divine events, but only a feature of fallible human credulity and testimony. Middleton further challenges the historical validity of miracles:

> In a word, to submit our belief implicitly and indifferently, to the mere source of authority, in all cases, whether miraculous or natural, without any rule of discerning the credible from the incredible, might support indeed the faith, as it is called, but would certainly destroy the use of all history; by leading us into perpetual errors, and possessing our minds with invincible prejudices, and false notions both of men and things.[14]

Moreover, the scriptural account of miracles, Middleton maintains, represents the result of the manipulation of the biblical texts by the early church fathers, who altered passages for their own purposes and entered corruptions into the Word. Middleton assails all those who had a hand in composing the Gospels, much as Paine would impugn the scriptural scribes as men "of a weak mind . . . void of reason and common sense . . . in want of judgment . . . from whose foolish reasonings, both in religion and morality, whole books have been compiled." Middleton allies the early gospel writers with "Magicians, Necromancers, or Conjurors," who trafficked in "performing miracles, foretelling future events," and summoning "the Souls of the dead."[15]

Orthodox defenders of Holy Writ had always argued that such representations of the fire, the lamb, the chariot, and the like were real. Skeptics like Middleton assumed that such figures were inventions, given elaborate and seemingly divine aspects by the religious establishment for the sake of enforcing superstitious belief. For Middleton, the books of the Bible are "human" documents just as are the ancient pagan writings of the same time.

Middleton's book and Hume's essay "Of Miracles" in *An Enquiry Concerning Human Understanding* (1748) were the two most formidable denunciations of miracles published in the eighteenth century. Edward Gibbon was profoundly influenced by Middleton's book,[16] and Paine as well seems to have known something of its arguments before writing *The Age of Reason.*

Also of interest to Paine is the issue of how the "human" documents of the New Testament were sanctioned as divine by the Christian church. In a footnote he refers to "Boulanger's 'Life of Paul', written in French" (1:586n), and thus provides another clue to the dependence of his biblical criticism on certain authorities.

The book Paine attributes to Nicolas-Antoine Boulanger (1722–59) is *Examen critique de la vie de saint Paul* (Paris, 1770), which was published in England as the *Critical Examination of the Life of St. Paul* (1823). The particular volume he used appeared in Boulanger's *Oeuvres*, which saw several editions in the 1770s through the 1790s. *Examen critique* may be based generally on a manuscript composed by Peter Annet (1693–1769),[17] a minor author of writings on deism and the new thought of his time. Whether or not this detail is true, the work as we have it is most likely an extensive revision by Paul Henri Thiry, Baron d'Holbach (1723–89) and his coterie, who often referred to themselves as *la boulangerie*. This group routinely recomposed Boulanger's writings, all of which appeared posthumously, including his *Le Christianisme dévoilé, ou Examen des principes et des effets de la Religion chrétienne* (1767; American edition 1795). The prolific Holbachean clique had a profound influence on French skepticism toward Scripture,[18] a skepticism Paine encountered through his intimate participation in French culture and history.

In an extended footnote concerning "the authenticity of the New Testament," Paine cites *Examen critique* on various sects or "parties": in "about the year 400" the Corinthians, Marcionists, and Encratites (Christian sects) were aware of the "imperfections, errors, and contradictions" in the books of the New Testament (1:587n). The Apostle Paul and his cohorts, Paine reports, "inserted in the Scriptures of our Lord many things . . . not written by himself, nor by his apostles" (1:586). Relatedly, in a passage anticipating Paine's citation of Faustus, *Examen critique* reports:

Faustus, the Manichean, said on the subject of the Gospels, that they had been composed a long time after the Apostles, by some obscure individuals, who fearing that faith would not be given to histories of facts with which they must have been acquainted, published under the name of the Apostles their own writings, so filled with anecdotes and discordant relations and opinions, that we can find in them neither connection nor agreement with themselves.[19]

The Gospels were, therefore, replete with corrupt emendations added to them later; it was the "spirit of party" that humanly determined the books of the New Testament but nonetheless proclaimed them to be divinely authenticated.

For the *coterie holbachique*, as represented in *Examen critique,* Paul was a passionately zealous, ambitious, and unscrupulous man. Tired of his youthful work as a tent-maker, he was attracted to the new religion and thereupon undertook to make himself prominent in that small and devout sect. He succeeded, Holbacheans maintained, by playing on "the nature of credulous, ignorant, and superstitious men." He exaggerated real events or invented fictional ones concerning miracles, such as the account of his conversion experience by a blinding light from heaven or his release from prison by doors magically opened by unseen hands. By this means Paul founded churches around the Mediterranean, made himself the center of their faith, and established some of its tenets, such as belief in a conversion experience and in salvation by faith, all in the name of what he claimed to be "authentic and divinely inspired." Paul's work of conversion, in the words of *la boulangerie,* was "very lucrative." The Holbacheans' summary judgment is severe: "Nothing is more injurious to the interests of truth, than the arrogance of an usurped authority."[20]

Thus, for the circle of Holbach, the authenticity of the first church, the subsequent sovereignty of the papacy established by Peter, and the legitimacy of the formidable Roman church all crumbled before this revelation of their foundation on a contrived and fabricated "human" scripture. The issue for *la boulangerie*, as for Paine and others, always arrived at the question of authority.

As suggested by the representative, and in their time well-known, examples of Toland, Jones, Collins, Tindal, Lardner, Middleton, and especially the *coterie holbachique,* biblical scholarship came of age in the eighteenth century and established the textual and historical emphasis of biblical studies today. In the eighteenth century, systematic methods were devised for clarifying, if not unraveling, the many problems of biblical texts that ever since antiquity had exhibited various anomalies. As the allusions to Livy and Tacitus in Jefferson's letter to Carr indicate, these systematic methods of the Neoclassical Age were informed by the application to scriptural studies of the recent advances made in the elucidation of similar problems relating to classical studies.

Paine lived at the very beginning of this enterprise, and had some insight into what it portended. There was already in place a substantial body of biblical attack and defense that Paine encountered, if not necessarily always or primarily by direct inquiry or reading, certainly by unavoidable contact with the general discussion pervasive in his milieu among skeptics and intellectuals, such as Jefferson in America and the revolutionists in France. The case Paine made would have been stronger and more effective had he presciently conceived what was to be understood later in biblical studies. But he knew much more of the pertinent precedent inquiries of his day than he admitted; and he knew enough to give his case some cogency, even if it was not entirely recognized in his own time.

Contemporaneous Biblical Commentary

Paine, as we saw in the second chapter, was in and out of London between 1787 and 1792. During this time, and while he was engaged in the controversy with Burke, Paine was a member of a group composed of his friends and defenders. Joseph Johnson (1738–1809), for one, had published *Rights of Man,* for which he would be found guilty of libel; later he would learn what it would cost him to publish seditious works by radical literati such as William Hazlitt, William Godwin, Horne Tooke, Mary Wollstonecraft, William Wordsworth, and Samuel Taylor Coleridge.[21] Paine was entertained at the home of Johnson, also the publisher of the *Analytical Review,* as well as at the home of Thomas Christie (1761–96), the essayist who edited that periodical for November 1790. Johnson's *Monthly Review* presented a distinctly dissenting point of view in matters of religion that paralleled the opinions expressed in his *Analytical Review.* Either directly or incidentally, articles and reviews in both of these journals raised exegetical concerns. Moreover, at those dinner gatherings in Johnson's home, discussions of biblical criticism as well as of liberty and justice sometimes culminated in violent debate.

Johnson had employed William Blake (1757–1827) for many years. At one of those evening parties at Johnson's home Blake "refuted the profanity of Paine," apparently meaning Paine's antireligious comments. On 12 September 1792, again at Johnson's house, Paine poured forth such "inflammatory eloquence" that Blake feared that Paine would be arrested: "On Paine's rising to leave, Blake laid his hands on the orator's shoulder, saying, 'You must not go home, or you are a dead man!' and hurried him off on his way to France, whither he was now in any case bound, to take his seat as French legislator."[22]

Blake, who shared some of Paine's skepticism about certain social and religious matters, had privately communicated his belief that the Old Testament scriptures were "an Example of the wickedness & deceit of the Jews & were written as an Example of the possibility of Human Beastliness in all its branches." In certain books of the Old Testament Blake found that "the destruction of the Canaanites by Joshua was the Unnatural design of wicked men. . . . To Extirpate a nation by means of another is as wicked as to destroy an individual by means of another individual." While he thought the Bible the greatest literary work of the "Western tradition," Blake, nonetheless, maintained that it was full of evil, a criticism he, in fact, also applied to all poetry. "Who Dare defend either the Acts of Christ or the Bible Unperverted[?]" Blake mused, concluding that "to defend the Bible . . . would cost a man his life," that is to say, his spiritual potentiality. During the controversy following the publication of Paine's *The Age of Reason,* Blake explicitly observed: "It appears to me Now that Tom Paine is a better Christian than the Bishop" Watson who attacked him.[23]

It is altogether likely that Paine also met Alexander Geddes (1737–1802), another member (with Blake and the Godwins) of Joseph Johnson's social circle. Geddes was a chief reviewer of recent biblical scholarship and criticism for Johnson's *Analytical Review* between 1788 and 1791. Even in the unlikely event that Paine never met Geddes personally, he would have encountered (before he left for France in 1792) the latter's writing in the *Analytical Review,* copies of which circulated among Johnson's friends. Geddes, after all, was writing on a subject of manifest interest to Paine at that time.

Geddes, who had been trained in French hermeneutics in Paris (the center of activity for the *coterie holbachique*), had been invited by the Catholic hierarchy in England to prepare a translation of the Bible. A first sketch of this undertaking appeared in 1780 under the title *Idea of a New Version of the Holy Bible, for the Use of the English Catholics.* Geddes intended to translate from the Vulgate while he used the Douay Version of the Bible as a basis for his work.

Later, in *Prospectus for a New Translation of the Holy Bible* (1786), Geddes argued that the received biblical texts were corrupt because they all derived from unreliable base texts. He maintained that the foundational Hebrew text, the Masoretic Bible, was a heteroglot work and, hence, did not reflect some original and pure inspiration. The other early texts, the Greek Septuagint and the Latin Vulgate, were obviously secondary and equally required critical investigation. A "new translation" could be produced only by returning to the original Hebrew documents, which would have to be critically examined and purified. Specifically concerning the Pentateuch, Geddes insisted on a return to the Samaritan Pentateuch as "a far more faithful representative of the prototype than any other masoretic copy at this day extant."[24]

Geddes's point about the authenticity of the Bible was informed by two general principles: that the texts of Scripture must be examined in the light of human reason, especially since they were, fundamentally and historically, human documents; and that these texts must be studied in the context of their composition and transmission. In short, the books of the Bible had been written in time and by persons who reflected their specific time. It mattered, for instance, that the Jews in the age of Isaiah were different from their ancestors in the age of Moses, Samuel, and David. Geddes thus concluded that the variant writings throughout the Old Testament showed that the Bible was fully a human document, not a divine one.

Geddes defended his contention by demonstrating that the Bible "has been more frequently copied than any other writing, and too often copied by ignorant and careless apographists."[25] More pointedly, Geddes affirmed that "the Pentateuch, in its present form, was not written by Moses," but by someone in the land of Canaan, and most probably at Jerusalem, and sometime not before the reign of David but after that of Hezekiah. Furthermore, the Pentateuch "has not come down to us in its full integrity, nor without alterations." Indeed, the Pentateuch, "reduced in its present form in the reign of Solomon," is a compilation

> from ancient documents, some of which were coeval with Moses, and some even anterior to Moses. Whether all of these were written records, or many of them only oral traditions, it would be rash to determine. It is my opinion that the Hebrews had no written documents before the days of Moses.

In *Prospectus for a New Testament Translation,* published before his edition of the Bible, Geddes put the issue clearly and succinctly:

> Two rival peoples, the Jews and the Samaritans, have preserved separate exemplars of [Genesis], in different characters. . . . We also have fragments of three . . . Greek versions, and a Chaldee paraphrase, of uncertain date. We have a Syriac translation. . . . In the Fourth century we have a Latin version by St. Jerome.[26]

In the preface to his translation of the Old Testament, Geddes went further in his analysis of the Pentateuch. There he outlined the so-called fragmentary or documentary theory of the biblical texts. This theory proposed that the Bible was a heterogeneous collection of materials gathered together at different times by different scribes. Geddes stated openly: "I constantly set aside the idea of inspiration, and consider the historical part of the Pentateuch as a mere human composition." By repeating some of the points he had made in the preface to his *Prospectus,* he again affirmed that "the Pentateuch was not written by Moses"; "it was written in the land of Canaan and most probably at Jerusalem; not before the reign of David, and after that of Hezekiah, but in the pacific reign of Solomon." In the Pentateuch, Geddes further declared, there are passages of "a posterior date, of a posterior interpolation" to the original scribal collection of the early books. In his preface, Geddes went so far as to treat the history of the Fall of Man as a mere fable and, as well, to stress the unsavory ferocity of the Israelites in killing their neighbors.

The first volume of Geddes's translation of the Bible appeared in London in 1792, the second in 1797.[27] The incomplete work contains Genesis to Chronicles and the book of Ruth. Behind the abandonment of this project was not only the fact that Geddes had consulted the Douay as well as the Vulgate versions as the basis of his own texts, but also the fact that he had consulted "the great mass of various readings, collected by biblical critics," so that "the true reading may be ascertained."[28] Geddes's radical approach to textual criticism and his frank admission of variant readings was influential[29] and provoked the hostility of both Catholics and Protestants.[30]

Although Paine developed his own scheme of inquiry to show the discrepancies in the biblical narratives, his interest in how its parts or strands differ in relation to each other corresponds to Geddes's view, as typically stated in the preface to his translation of the Bible, that the scriptural texts dramatically exhibit lacunae and discontinuities. Geddes demoted many scriptural elements to mere narrative increment or tissue, put there by a later scribe or copyist to suit the taste of his time or his culture. Moreover, there were hidden elements, certain instructions and overlays, which determine the meaning of a passage; accordingly, there could be an idea, a submerged human interest, or (in modern terms) a mythos hidden beneath the narrative surface.

In some sense, and it may well have been a rather direct influence, Geddes's arguments figured in Paine's exposition of the slips and misadventures in the "divinely inspired" Bible. At the very least, Geddes's authority and outspokenness served to license Paine's certainty and candor in speaking on his own of the Bible. Geddes's "rational" quest for what he called "the bare literal meaning" corresponded precisely to Paine's "rational" effort to reveal the truth obscured beneath the surface of the biblical narratives.[31] This surface could be cleansed, they both maintained, by removing the overlay of priestly or scribal additions; then a literal, clear text would be revealed.

In *The Age of Reason,* furthermore, Paine would share Geddes's opinion that Genesis is an edited collection of mythological narratives that have their basis in the cultural, rather than the divine, history of the ancient Hebrews. When Geddes turned his attention to the Fall, he detected "an excellent *mythologue*" reflecting the ideas of primitive Judaism;[32] and Paine, too, would speak of "mythologue" and of "Church Mythologists" in *The Age of Reason* (1:467, 469–70). *Mythologue* was a term that Geddes, Paine, and their contemporaries applied to ancient texts, pagan and biblical alike, which encoded specific cultural ideas or attitudes—what we today speak of as *folkways.* Geddes and Paine agreed with the *coterie holbachique* that the primitive parts of the Bible represented a simpleminded, superstitious people; for it endowed certain prophets and seers with magical embodiments, all of which were merely manifestations of natural forces at work in the world. Both men understood, moreover, that the magic of fire, sword, water, altar, and mountaintop in the Bible were identical to the manifestations of these same features in ancient Babylonian and Greek accounts.

Both Geddes and Paine, like their contemporaries Godwin and Wollstonecraft, were committed to a rational approach to religion and politics, and in this respect they both contributed to the manner of Toland, Jones, Collins, Tindal, Lardner, and the Holbachean clique, their prominent predecessors in biblical criticism. Finally, as we turn our attention in the next chapter to *The Age of Reason,* it may also be appropriate to bear in mind that Paine's insistence on the way religion is used as a prop for those in political power corresponds to a feature of Geddes's work. Geddes's arguments and his translation of the Bible had more than a religious purpose; they also implied throughout (as the writings of *la boulangerie* and of Blake did as well) a sense of political mission.

4

Paine Reads
the Bible

Paine intended *The Age of Reason* to present what he called "the theology that is true" (1:464). His own faith, he professed, contained two articles: "I believe in one God, and no more; . . . and I believe that religious duties consist in doing justice, loving mercy, and endeavoring to make our fellow creatures happy" (1:464). For Paine, the Deity is worthy of belief and worship, not as He is described in the Bible, but as He is made known, represented, in the ever-widening knowledge of science.

The Age of Reason, as Paine affirmed, was designed to counter the atheism coming as an effect of the French Revolution and to clarify a belief in God based on "true" religion, free from cant and superstition, and based on the uniform laws of nature and human thought. The "Almighty lecturer" speaks "universally to man" in "all nations" on "all worlds" through the "universal language" of his creation (1:482–83).

Paine conceded (1:485), however, that occasionally the Bible conveyed something of this divine revelation, particularly in the book of Job and in the Nineteenth Psalm (as paraphrased in Joseph Addison's well-known hymn). Paine also affirmed his belief in the person of Jesus as a good man who lived and died at a certain time in history. Paine accepted the Bible as a history of a people over a long span of time, a history of the great effects of certain patriarchs on the lives of their people. Paine recognized elements of truth in Scripture that were, he thought, acceptable to persons of reason.

Nevertheless, to appreciate these features of the Bible, Paine maintained, it is necessary to penetrate through the pretensions, flaws, discrepancies, and errors in its narrative. Only then could the Word have any place or pertinence in the human future that Paine prophesied. It was to this end, as a requirement for his underlying political agenda, that Paine set out in *The Age of Reason* to reveal the true nature of Scripture.

Tradition and Authority in Biblical Interpretation

As we observed in the last chapter, for centuries old questions about Scripture had been raised by scholars, exegetes, and commentators: How had the Bible come to be? Who wrote it? Can it be rightly called "the Book of God," or was it the work of human hands? Paine had his own answers to these long-considered questions. Although, as we also saw in chapter 3, he had been exposed to something of this legacy, he indicated that he had no need for it, that he would inquire into these and other matters on his own, authorized only by the universal human attribute of "reason and philosophy" (1:467).

One truism of this long-established and generally unquestioned heritage (at least from Luther onward in Protestant thought) held that "scripture doth best interpret itself." Holy Writ contains everything necessary for its understanding. All that is needed to read and perceive its truth is a humble inquirer, enlightened (some would say "saved") by the very Word itself and the spirit of God acting in and through the Word. As authorities and lay readers averred, Scripture requires no exegesis or commentary to be efficacious.[1]

This long Protestant tradition, that the Word explains itself, prevailed side by side with a different idea, the Pauline notion that Scripture can be difficult and obscure. The Bible could reveal itself only because it was divine in origin; but this divine origin necessarily meant that the truth scripturally revealed to postlapsarian humanity must finally be an ultimate truth far beyond the limits of human language (the means) and human understanding (the end). Thus, according to this second tradition, even if the Word accommodates the language and ways of human thinking, there always must be a significant distance between its divine origin and purpose, on the one hand, and its human reception and understanding, on the other. This sense of the Bible as a deep and complex mystery, as Paine himself perceived it, persisted together with the tradition affirming that Scripture readily interprets itself to human readers.

Also, tradition taught that Holy Writ offers its divine teaching in human verses, that is, in small compact pieces. Whether single verses, chapters, or books, these pieces are, nonetheless, parts of a uniform whole. Believing in such an association, interpreters followed a course through these small segments, units of thoughts, and little increments to disclose this whole. Therefore, tradition held, people should read Scripture—telling what the Book opens to them and what they are privileged to know—by following in order the compact segments and then by speaking in their own voice. Their voice is empowered, not by itself, but by the form and power of the Bible, with its every unit in place leading to the complete text as designed and executed when the Word itself was revealed.

But how had every word of Scripture been given at that revelation, and how had every word been put in place just as it is printed in the Bible? And how can the verses in their divine order be made clearly understandable as revelation if human comprehension depends on a translation of this revelation into the inadequate terms of everyday speech? Such awareness of the need for an extreme translation to bring revelation of the divine Word to human words included, as well, an awareness of the need for an arduous retranslation of these human words to render the revelation of the divine Word. Obviously, Holy Writ, for all its surface simplicity and ordinariness, is not plainness all through, as is suggested by the notion that Scripture best interprets itself.

Paine made use of both points of view. First, in a disingenuous gesture, he seemed to accept the tradition that Scripture best interprets itself. He affirmed at one point, "The evidence I shall produce is contained in the book itself; I will not go out of the Bible for proof against the supposed authenticity of the Bible" (1:531). But, second, when he added in the next sentence that "false testimony is always good against itself," he suggested the other biblical tradition concerning Scripture as a deep and complex mystery that is not plainness all through.

The latter tradition prevails in *The Age of Reason,* with the primary difference that Paine emphasized, with a vengeance, the distance between divine revelation and human expression. For him, finally, the Bible should be approached solely in the light of what such a distance implies: not only that the divinity of Scripture should be doubted, but also that its commentary should be empirically assessed primarily in terms of contemporary thought and human behavior. Paine read Holy Writ the same way he read a historical narrative, a moral argument, or a social or political treatise of his own time—each of which, in fact, he assumed Scripture to be. It could, then, like any narrative, argument, or treatise, be answered and countered.

Such an approach naturally led to Paine's reconsideration of those centuries-old questions: Who wrote the Bible? Are the names attributed to its individual books accurate designators of their authors? If Holy Writ is both divine revelation and human expression, how did it come to be in the form it now has? When did it receive this form?

From the outset Paine alleges that the Bible has no claim to divine authorship or authority. He concedes that while some of its parts seem to have divine sanction, equal importance cannot be given to most of the scriptural narratives. Some of these narratives, he is sure, are authentic historical records, and many of the prophecies, poems, and wise sayings express the age in which they were composed.

The Bible is, for Paine, a collection of various kinds of writings that resemble similar assemblages by other people of ancient times. Fragments of history in some written form, documents, poems, declarations, speeches, and various certificates of governmental action comprised the original records that the Jews kept throughout times of war and settlement. There was as well, in Paine's view, something of a long-surviving original narrative—including stories, poems, and sayings—that had been orally transmitted from one generation to another and perhaps crudely recorded in the Bible.

Because Paine sees a glaring discrepancy between this original simple narrative and what (to him) quite obviously was editorially manipulated and distorted later, he assumes a two-stage composition of the scriptural documents. The book of Ruth, for example, strikes Paine as essentially a simple folktale concerning a young woman who worked in the fields of a wealthy man, was taken to his bed, and eventually became his wife; but at some later stage this story was made to account for the beginning of a generation of Israelite kings who represent the founding of David's royal line. Paine concludes that, in this instance as throughout the Old Testament, the later "compilers were ignorant" of the identity of "the first narrators" and "confounded the writings of different authors with each other" (1:552–53). These later editors elaborated on early folktales to give them an allegorical and sacral significance. Through this endeavor these editors sought to inspire the Jewish people with a sense of their religious and national destiny; but they also connived for personal advantage in their management of the scriptural texts. That such corrupting *political* intentions inform much of Scripture is a critical feature of Paine's argument in *The Age of Reason.*

Paine accordingly assumes that he can read the Old Testament both for what "the first narrators" had seen or known, and for what they could not have seen or known but what was credited to them afterward. Despite Paine's hostility toward these original narrators, toward Moses and other famous Old Testament patriarchal figures, he, in some sense, imaginatively identifies with them, as if he too were a first recorder. Like them, he sets out to tell the truth. In another sense, he imaginatively identifies with the later "compilers," with the important difference that (in his opinion) he demystifies, rather than mystifies, the texts. Like these later priests or scribes, Paine discloses the form and character of the scriptural records.

Primarily he discloses how the "contradictions in time, place, and circumstances that abound in the books" were the handiwork of three different but related designers: the "Bible-makers," the "chronologists," and the "compilers" (1:531, 551). The Bible-makers put together the separate books as they were given an early and perhaps tentative form. The chronologists put the books in their order according to a design of history that the Bible seemed to reveal to them. And, as we saw, the compilers edited the text in its present form. In Paine's opinion, each group was unaware of what the other was doing, although the Bible-makers had not completed their undertaking when the chronologists set about their task, and although while these two groups were still making their final decisions and additions, the compilers entered the process. Besides numerous contradictions and discrepancies, this confusion of hands strikes Paine also as evidence of fraud. The books of the Bible, Paine concludes, were made to promise far more than was ever intended at first and were made to perpetuate false beliefs for the purpose of controlling human minds and maintaining a tyrannical state.

The Historical Books of the Old Testament

In demystifying the Old Testament, Paine conducts two inquiries. The first concerns the accuracy of dating; the second concerns the attribution of authorship.

Paine reasons that the Old Testament chronology should successfully withstand the test of mathematical judgment. Besides the fact that the fourth book is titled Numbers, the Scriptures evidence throughout a scrupulous concern with such matters as the populations of neighbors, the size of triumphant or slain armies, and the number of sheaves of grain. Aided by Ussher's chronology (which, as we noted in chapter 3, seemed to many to be a part of Holy Writ itself),[2] Paine tests the accuracy of the Bible by what he assumes is Scripture's own testimony.

Paine establishes two dates central to the biblical record: the death of Moses in 1,451 B.C. and the fall of Jerusalem and the Babylonian Captivity in 588 B.C. These dates, Paine contends, are reliable because of evidence from ancillary pagan commentaries; hence, these dates can serve as an accurate measure for a biblical chronology. Subtracting the date of Moses' death from earlier dates, Paine deduces that the historical placement of the Israelite patriarchs is in all respects correct.

While assessing the accuracy of these dates, Paine makes two particularly noteworthy mistakes. He places the death of Joshua 331 years after the death of Moses, resulting in an improbable statistic for the duration of

Joshua's life that conflicts with the scriptural report that Joshua died twenty years after Moses' passing. Likewise, after reviewing the chronology of Judges, Paine sets the difference between chapters 16 and 17–21 as twenty-eight years, whereas the scriptural dating amounts to 286 years.

Concerning his other primary inquiry, the attribution of authorship, Paine especially focuses on the Pentateuch. From the outset Paine assumes that Moses could not have written its books:

> They were not written in the time of Moses, nor till several hundred years afterward; . . . they are no other than an attempted history of the life of Moses, and of the times in which he is said to have lived, . . . written by some very ignorant and stupid pretenders to authorship several hundred years after the death of Moses, as men now write histories of things that happened, or are supposed to have happened, several hundred or several thousand years ago. (1:521)

The Pentateuch, particularly the account of Creation, Paine reports, owed much to its being based on "a tradition which the Israelites had among them before they came out of Egypt; and after their departure from that country they put it [the story of the Creation] at the head of their history" (1:473). One reason why an Egyptian legend appears at the beginning of an Israelite history, and was assigned to Moses, Paine deduces, was that this patriarch "was not an Israelite," but had "been educated among the Egyptians, who were a people as well skilled in science, and particularly in astronomy, as any people of their day" (1:474). [3]

Paine also adduces that the style of the Pentateuch represents a "person speaking of Moses" in the third person. "Any man might speak of himself in that manner," Paine reasons, but it cannot be supposed "that it is Moses who speaks" concerning his own meekness (Numb. 12:3) or his own death and burial in the land of Moab (Deut. 34:5–6) "without rendering Moses truly ridiculous and absurd." On the basis of these details and other "fallibilities," Paine concludes that the Pentateuch was written by "some Jewish priest, who lived . . . at least three hundred and fifty years after the time of Moses" (1:521–24). [4]

After enumerating other "fallibilities"—including references to Dan and to Israelite kings that make Mosaic authorship impossible—Paine turns from the Pentateuch to the subsequent historical books of the Old Testament. He claims that Job is the oldest book in the Bible, that it contains astronomical allusions foreign to the Israelites, and that, as we noted in chapter 3, it was originally a Gentile work "translated from another language into Hebrew" (1:547). The historical books from

Samuel, through Kings and Chronicles, Paine indicates, betray in every chapter the haphazard joint work of their editors.[5] The Psalms, too, Paine affirms in correspondence with contemporary scholarship, were not all written by King David, but "by different song-writers, who lived at different times" from the Israelites' occupation of the Holy Land to the Babylonian Captivity (1:549). Nor were the Canticles or Proverbs, with matter clearly dating after the death of Solomon, entirely composed by that "worn-out debauchee" with "seven hundred wives and three hundred concubines" (1:550).

The Prophetic Books of the Old Testament

Paine's consideration of these historical books is surpassed by his interest in the prophetic books of the Old Testament, "the writings of the Jewish poets" that "deserve a better fate than that of being bound up . . . with the trash that accompanies them, under the absurd name of the Word of God" (1:477).[6] He constructs a chronological table and assigns to each prophet his time and place according to that determining date, 588 B.C. when Jerusalem was destroyed. By subtracting this date from the number assigned to each prophet, Paine arranged all the prophets from Isaiah to Malachi, from the year 760 to 397 B.C. He erred in assigning the dates of Hosea by one hundred years, of Amos by two years, Obadiah by ten years, Habbakuk by four years and Haggai by eighteen years.

Paine registers a special interest in the books of Isaiah and Jeremiah, which were the prophecies most highly regarded by Jews and Christians throughout the centuries. Both, Paine argues, have been made to appear as prophecies inspired by God, but both reveal that they are only self-betraying and disordered assemblages—like "a bundle of newspapers" (1:556) —of anecdotes and scraps of historical accounts surviving by word-of-mouth or in priestly records. As a result, what might have been intended as prophecies in the original statements may have been clear to their composers (whoever they may have been), but the transcriptions of these prophecies with interpolated interpretations several centuries later were based on a language obscured during the Babylonian Captivity and on a confusion and mystery of meanings that were lost.

Paine's discussion of these two books is very detailed. Typical of his argument is his consideration of the prophecy of the virgin and child in Isaiah, which book also foretells that King Ahaz of Judah would defeat in battle two kings who challenged him. This prophecy, Paine is quick to point out, was wrong, and significantly wrong: "Ahaz was defeated and destroyed, a hundred and twenty thousand of his people were slaughtered, Jerusalem was plundered, and two hundred thousand women, and sons and daughters, carried into captivity" (1:555).[7]

The book of Jeremiah, Paine contends, is similarly plagued by "contradictory accounts" emerging from its origin in a "medley of detached, unauthenticated anecdotes" assembled later by some unknown and "stupid book-maker" (1:559): the prophet is imprisoned for being a spy in one verse, but for being a false prophet in another verse; the prophet predicts Nebuchadnezzar's slaughter of the inhabitants of Jerusalem, but they were spared and taken into captivity;[8] and the prophet reassures Zedekiah of his safety, but this king of Judah is mutilated and imprisoned until he dies.

Furthermore, Paine observes, if the prophecies in the Old Testament had indeed forecast the events of the New Testament, surely the writers of the Gospels would have made the connection. Yet no such clear association occurs, only vague implications. Paine suspects that the books of the prophets are not, after all, about prophecy.

When Paine considers who were the original personages whose sayings have been assembled, edited, interpreted, and distorted, he indicates that they were not in their time considered to be soothsayers. They were like the entertainers in medieval courts who told stories celebrating "the event of battle . . . or of a journey, or of [an] enterprise" (1:561), either in the past or in the future. They were seers not only in expressing hopeful expectations, but especially in composing verses; for the term *seer*, Paine asserts, meant poet as well as fortune-teller. Transmitted to later generations, these seers' elemental stories—"fictitious, and often extravagant, and not admissible in any other kind of writing than poetry" (1:475n)—acquired great importance as the various assemblers of the Bible embellished these simple, primitive narratives with profound religious and cultural implications.

In a very important move in his book, Paine argues that the composers of these original narratives were members of parties, akin to political alignments and factions in contemporary politics: "They prophesied for or against, according to the party they were with, as the poetical and political writers of the present day write in defense of the party they associate with against the other" (1:562). This alignment of the poet-prophets to parties became crucial after the death of Solomon, when the kingdom splintered into Israel and Judah. "Each party had its prophets, who abused and accused each other of being false prophets, lying prophets, impostors," Paine concludes; "the prophets of the party of Judah prophesied against the prophets of the party of Israel; and those of the party of Israel against those of Judah" (1:562).

This political dimension emerges somewhat differently in the books of Daniel and Ezekiel, which Paine allows were indeed written by the individuals named in their headings but which he disallows as prophecies.[9] Paine reads these two books as an effort by their captive authors to relate to their compatriots back in Jerusalem certain "political projects and opinions." They did so, however, "in obscure and metaphysical terms," and masqueraded their views and intentions as "dreams and visions" to evade detection by their captors. However "wild as . . . dreams and visions," Paine notes, these remarkable documents concealed the political hopes of a captured people for their restoration (1:564–65). Paine's reading of these books, like his reading of the Pentateuch as bearing *political* implications, is an important component in his agenda underlying the biblical commentary in *The Age of Reason.*

The New Testament

Paine also questions the authenticity of the New Testament. Whereas he allows that Jesus was indeed a "virtuous reformer and revolutionist" (1:469), he disallows everything else in the New Testament as a fiction perpetrated as divine inspiration by Jesus' followers long after his death. Finding discrepancies in the gospel account of Jesus' genealogy, Paine concludes that this genealogy is as much a fabrication as is the attribution of the Gospels to the names appearing at their headings. Since the Gospels are fictional, as the "impositions" of the Crucifixion, Resurrection, and Ascension particularly suggest, the Pauline epistles, dependent on these Gospels, are similarly suspect. Paine claims thereby to have shown that the Gospels were "forgeries" on the basis of evidence "extracted from the books themselves" (1:594).[10]

One of Paine's most outspoken, and perverse, conclusions is that none of the Four Gospels could have been composed before three hundred years after the death of Jesus (1:585–86). Instead of offering any evidence, he let this assertion stand as the well-supported conclusion of other authorities. Perhaps in reaching this conclusion he had in mind the First Council of the early church (Laodicea), which fixed the canon of Scripture in 363.[11] By dating the Gospels this late, Paine challenged their accuracy and their inspiration as divine expression. From the fourth century to the present, Paine believed, Christianity has been an imposition on credulous and trusting people.

The followers of Jesus at first were unaffected by priesthood, Paine speculates, but they had the example of Judaism, from which they had separated. Within a century or so, these Christians organized themselves much on the model of their religious predecessors, Jewish as well as pagan, in order to achieve a coherence and authority, both important to the survival of the new faith. Accordingly, Paine reports, they made Jesus, who was originally a simple man-founder of their faith, into a figure quite out of proportion to what he had been in real life, a figure now empowered with the ability to work miracles. This process of mystification included the attribution to Jesus of all manner of wonderful perquisites typical of a god: mysterious comings and goings, strange Orphic sayings, obscure hints, cryptic messages, magical workings, and divine descent. Now he had become the Messiah prophesied centuries before his time.

Thus, for Paine, the books of the New Testament are as replete with fable and superstition as are the books of the Old Testament. Although the first Christians lived in a time when certain rays of the light of reason illuminated the Greek and Roman world, they (like the people of classical antiquity) were still the victims of priests in league with rulers, both of whom enforced the worship of idols and gods as a way of sustaining their own very human power. Recalling similar observations about the scribal work in the Pentateuch and the role of the poetic seers in the prophetic books, this conclusion about the New Testament similarly touches on Paine's underlying political agenda in *The Age of Reason.*

The Question of Miracles and Political Power

Church authorities argued that the accounts of the miracles attributed to Jesus in the New Testament are trustworthy because they were either witnessed by persons who were present on the occasion or were recorded by intelligent persons not long afterward. One official version held that the evidence for miracles is identical to that for natural facts and events as experienced by people: both involve signs, actions, and results verifiable at the time of their occurrence by reliable witnesses close enough to the events to testify to their truth. Although miracles, by their nature, are in other ways separate from natural facts, nevertheless, authorities claimed, there is sufficient reason to trust those reported in the New Testament because of the sufficient number and the unbiased nature of the witnesses. In short, church spokesmen imputed a dual character to these divine and true gospel episodes: the events were extraordinary, but the persons reporting these events were not unusual, even if inspired.

What could be accepted as evidence for miracles in their own time, and what could be construed as evidence for miracles that could be sustained and believed in later times? Was that evidence the same or different? Orthodox authorities argued that the reasons for belief in miracles remained the same throughout time. Miracles were necessary, they indicated, not to excite wonder, but to herald and characterize the divine nature of the revelation contained in Christ's precepts and teachings. Consequently, the first baptism in the River Jordan required the appearance of a dove and the hearing of a voice; the celebration of the Last Supper required the transmutation of bread and wine; and the promise of eternal life required the death and resurrection of Jesus.

Nearly all the defenses of miracles and revealed religion depend on this principle: that the most enlightened moral system the world has ever known, Christianity, could have come into the world only in the way the biblical accounts provide. To deny the evidence for and the reliability of the New Testament accounts of miracles is to deny the claims for the Christic divine revelation they herald. Without this evidence, the Christian faith and its moral system disintegrate.

Of course, Paine denies the authenticity of this evidence. He advances arguments and language similar to those articulated by Conyers Middleton and the circle of Paul Henry Thiry, Baron d'Holbach, a few of whose main points we reviewed in chapter 3. Like Middleton, Paine asserts the function of mere human credulity in the biblical accounts of miracles, accounts composed by weak-minded narrators. Moreover, Paine repeats several of the related conclusions of the *coterie holbachique,* especially concerning Paul's invention of miraculous events to create a mystique about himself and his narratives. Paine and the clique of d'Holbach agree, too, that in the period when Christianity was gaining recognition in the Roman Empire and when it set about legitimatizing its power, self-aggrandizing church fathers altered and further corrupted the scriptural texts—mystified them with a sense of the miraculous—during councils of ecclesiastical legislation. "It was upon the vote of such men as Athanasius," Paine declared, "that the Testament was decreed to be the Word of God; and nothing can present to us a more strange idea than that of decreeing the word of God by vote" (1:594).

This last point is the final link in what is a chain of associations for Paine in *The Age of Reason.* In this scheme, the church fathers had exerted on the New Testament a corrupting priestly manipulation just as, before them, had the disciples of Jesus who themselves had followed the example of the scribes and prophets of the Old Testament. From the Pentateuch, through the books of the prophets, to the Gospels and epistles of the New Testament, and to the later interpretations of them by the church fathers, Paine contends, there has been one long and continuous history of priestly conspiracy to maintain a superstitious mystique in support of their own authority.

This authority has always meant worldly power over people, and so Paine is not surprised to find that these priests throughout time aligned themselves to parties, to the political forces of civil magistracy. In regard to the Judeo-Christian tradition, this alignment dated back to "the wretch" Moses, who "carried on wars . . . on the pretense of religion" (1:528), and to the prophets, who "prophesied for or against, according to the party they were with, as the poetical and political writers of the present day write in defense of the party they associate with against the other" (1:562). Jesus' followers inevitably followed this Judaic example, and this same pattern was continued by the early Christians and the church fathers, who (Paine believes) became allied with the civil power of the Roman Empire, under the emperor Constantine, when the first Council of Nicea was held in 325. From that time onward, the oppressive tyranny of church and state increasingly encroached on the natural liberties of the people of the West.

Through the invention of sacred texts, stories, and legends, as well as of holy places, rites, rituals, and ceremonies, priests and magistrates mystified their own power in an effort to command unquestioned reverence and obedience from a credulous multitude "enslaved" by this claim to divine right by both their religious and civil guardians. Paine's claim here about biblical mystification recalls a political point in *Rights of Man*, which specifically addresses how the ruling class has always taken "care to represent government as a thing made up of mysteries, which only [they] themselves understood," and has always aimed to convince their property-like inherited subordinates to "believe that government is some wonderful mysterious thing" (1:361, 375). Thomas Hobbes (1588–1679) had made a similar observation in *Leviathan* (1651), which reports that the Bible derives its power from the decree of Christian rulers, who demand that the Sacred Book be regarded as divine law. Revealing this connection between church and state throughout time is the real design behind Paine's religious commentary in *The Age of Reason*. In this work he assails scriptural authority because this authority seemed to him to be the dubious foundation of both religion and state in the Western world.

Pertinent hints of this central concern typically emerge in Paine's language when he fashions such expressions as "the amphibious fraud" and "the adulterous connection of church and state" to expose how the political "sword," used to acquire "power and revenue," is the main instrument of "this impious thing called revealed religion" (1:465, 467, 586, 596). The most telling moments, however, significantly frame

Paine's book. In "The Author's Profession of Faith" he says that his work is "exceedingly necessary" because "of the false systems of government and false theology," because the "institutions of churches" are "human inventions" designed to "monopolize power and profit" (1:464). And in his "Conclusion" Paine recalls this very point—the underlying point of his book—by bluntly writing, "It has been the scheme of the Christian Church, and of all the other invented systems of religion, to hold man in ignorance of the Creator, as it is of Governments to hold man in ignorance of his rights. The systems of the one are as false as those of the other, *and are calculated for mutual support*" (1:601; emphasis added). What could be clearer than this revelation of Paine's intent, of the rationale behind his subversion of the authority of Scripture, on whose imputed authenticity the Western church and state were and are founded?

The Authority of a Dismembered Hand

The issue of authority, as we have seen, is an abiding concern in Paine's major works. In *Common Sense* and the *Crisis* papers he deposes the sovereignty of monarchies; in *Rights of Man* he deposes the legitimacy of aristocratic monarchical minions such as Edmund Burke; in *The Age of Reason* he deposes the supremacy of priests, from Moses to clerics and theologians at the end of the eighteenth century. Now and then, as we have seen, the earlier works anticipate the later book; and in fact from *Common Sense* to *The Age of Reason* Paine progresses from dealing with "appearances[, which] are so capable of deceiving" (1:508), to scrutinizing origins, which are buried in the past. In attacking the authenticity of Scripture, Paine tries to uproot, expose, and destroy these hidden origins of the power attributed to church and state, that "amphibious fraud."

But from where did Paine derive his own empowerment to pontificate on Scripture? We noted, in chapter 3, his exposure to the ideas of several previous French and English commentators and to prevalent notions circulating within the international intellectual milieu of his time. But such an encounter was hardly sufficient, and Paine claimed (albeit disingenuously) it was utterly unnecessary (although in infrequent lapses he mentions scriptural authorities sympathetic to his position). In resorting to the dual, contrary biblical traditions holding that Holy Writ is its own best interpreter and that the Word could be difficult and obscure, Paine proclaimed (as we remarked) his autonomy in reading Scripture: "The evidence I shall produce is contained in the book itself; I will not go out of the Bible for proof against the supposed authenticity of the Bible" (1:531).

As we have also seen in *Common Sense* and *Rights of Man*, however, such claims to self-fathering are fraught with paradox, and this paradox reaches a fascinating epitome in Paine's strategies for self-authorization in *The Age of Reason*.

Some of Paine's maneuvers in this book recall those in his earlier writings. There is, first, his enablement through opposition, the instating of himself by virtue of the substantiality of his priestly opponents, without whom his voice would have no cause to perform, indeed no *raison d'être*. There is, second, his use of the mechanism of transference or displacement when he insists on and repeats his claim to write by the light (the Inner Light, as it were) of "reason and philosophy," even if this formulation, as a mere abstract assertion, lacks any evidence of the empiricality imputed to it in Paine's invocations. In a related maneuver, reminiscent of a strategy in *Rights of Man*, Paine consigns the authorization of his book of "consolation" to the historical moment—"the times and the subject demand it be done" (1:472)—and to the example of others who have met peoples' need for "consolation" at this moment:

> As several of my colleagues and others of my fellow-citizens of France, have given me the example of making their voluntary and individual profession of faith, I also will make mine; and I do this with all that sincerity and frankness with which the mind of man communicates with itself. (1:464)

As these strategies, and his ever-so-subtle sympathetic identification with the "the reformer[s] and revolutionist[s]" Jesus and Luther (1:469, 495) suggest, Paine's claim of independent self-communication, his reiteration of sole reliance on pure reason, does not, in fact, prevail. Nor does he successfully demonstrate his claim to be his own patriarch or priest in his "own mind," as his "own church," where "almost all the knowledge" that he has acquired has derived from the revelation (from whence?) of "thoughts . . . that bolt into [his] mind of their own accord" (1:464, 497). Such an effort to appropriate extreme independence falters because, as our Introduction indicated, the assertion of self-authorization is a performance always caught between dependency and autonomy; it is an act always conflicted by rage against the established priestly patriarchy and by fear of the self-inflicted, potentially suicidal wound of becoming (as Paine himself pejoratively uses the expression) "altogether fatherless" (1:534)—that is, without authenticity.

In *The Age of Reason* Paine attempts another mode of the mechanism of transference, one that he had briefly suggested in *Rights of Man* and one that pretends a sort of hermetic closure with himself, as if an otherwise elusive sense of autonomy has indeed been attained. In this gambit, Paine grounds his authority on his previous performance, in effect telling his audience, "All of you already know who I am, what I stand for." And that this audience did know mattered, of course; but Paine's recourse to this manner is nonetheless a rhetorical tactic for self-authorization. "You will do me the justice to remember, that I have always strenuously supported the right of every man to his own opinion" (1:463), contains phrasing not only looking backward ("remember") but also forward to what is to come: Paine's controversial opinion. This comment at once asserts dependence on the past and assertion of independence from it, a gesture recalling the same dilemma in Paine's earlier writings, which overtly, at least, declare the need for a complete emancipation from the past but always fail to achieve it. That the authority invoked from the past is Paine's own authority does not dismiss the conflicted implications of the stratagem itself.

This curious backward-and-forward looping is even more evident when Paine evokes, for the purpose of authorizing his present controversial discourse, the reader's memory of his role in the American Revolution (the past) and especially of *Common Sense,* falsely said to be "the first work [he] ever did publish," as the foreground of *The Age of Reason:* "I believe I should never have been known in the world as an author on any subject whatsoever had it not been for the affairs of America" (1:496–97). Covertly he instates himself as already "known"; and this worldly reputation, dependently grounded not only on his own past performance, but also on the substantial past success of a whole nation, authenticates Paine's present authorship/authority in *The Age of Reason.*

If such reflexivity seems on first encounter to signify a sort of hermeneutic of self suggesting an autonomous authority, on second thought it reveals a dependency on a past as witnessed by others, who must remember Paine, that alleged autonomous self, in a double regression to critical precedent events: the publication of his book, itself founded on the evident substantiality of the new American republic. This contestatory engagement of dependency on the past and freedom in the present in Paine's authorship of *The Age of Reason* registers in another form as well, the paradox that has been evident in his previous writings.

This paradox inheres in all of the tactics for authorization to which Paine resorts. First, his enablement through opposition: if Paine successfully deposes all priestcraft, there would then be an erasure of the substantial cause of the performance of his voice, which in any event is defined (and thereby curiously identified with) priestly fraud. Second, the resort to the abstract assertion of reason and rights amounts to a nonevidentiary empiricality, an absence, which in effect opens a void behind Paine's speech. Third, the reference to the late eighteenth century for authorization results, in effect, in a vacancy because all times are transient and, worse still, become the very pernicious past that Paine seeks to drive out of existence, even out of human memory. Fourth, references to the example of others' work and others' lives disable claims to autonomy, not only by yoking Paine's present performance to the always corrupt past to be buried, but also by eradicating any sense of the individuality, uniqueness, even substantiality of Paine's voice. Fifth, and most fascinating, the invocation of *Common Sense* raises a number of instances of this paradox of erasure.

Paine published *Common Sense* anonymously, perhaps a clue to a hesitation at that time to take responsibility for the authority literally asserted in his book. An anonymous author is, in effect, an absent author; yet in *The Age of Reason* this "authorless" *Common Sense* is invoked as authorizing. This maneuver is all the more puzzling because in *The Age of Reason* Paine specifically disparages anonymity, as if he forgets that he used it previously himself in *Common Sense*, the very book he now calls on to authenticate his biblical commentary. "The book of Genesis is anonymous and without authority," he states, repeating this point later when he speaks of the two works attributed to Samuel as "anonymous and without authority" like "all [the] former books" of the Bible (1:526, 535). This attribution of the absence of authority subverts Paine's strategy of predicating his new book on his old anonymous book.

This predication evinces another dilemma. In deriving authenticity from *Common Sense* Paine implies something positive about the durability of language. Although he does suggest in one place that writing is as close to immortality as one can come (1:591), he contrarily notes that languages die (1:491), that print is corruptible (1:585n), and that words are always an unreliable vehicle for expressing reality and truth. For Paine, it is not just that "the Word of God cannot exist in any written or human language" because of, among other reasons, "the continually progressive change to which the meaning of words is subject"; for Paine, "human language is [always] local and changeable, and is therefore incapable of being used as the means of unchangeable and universal information" (1:477, 482; cf. 483). Oddly, Paine has appropriated Burke's sense of his opponents' language as Babel-like, which we observed in chapter 2. Paine's notion of the inability of language to convey "universal information" annihilates his claim that *The Age of Reason* is based on and expresses "reason and philosophy"; and it does violence to its other prop of displaced authorization, the invocation of *Common Sense*.

The stratagem of recalling *Common Sense* as an enabling agent for Paine's proclamations in *The Age of Reason* is vexed by more than Paine's attack, in the latter book, on the efficacy of language in relation to reality and truth. As we saw in chapter 1, in *Common Sense* Paine confiscated regal scriptural authority to support his assertions. A paradox occurs when Paine resorts to a book credited by its arrogation of scriptural authority to authenticate his performance in a book explicitly deposing "Bible authority" (1:517). Paine's effort to close hermetically with himself, by privileging his authority on the basis of previous authorship in this instance, enters a logical void.

All of these conflicted strategies, at once enabling and disabling the claims for authority in *The Age of Reason,* dramatize the stagelike middle ground between independence and dependence on which Paine is necessarily situated. And it is at this site of spectacle that the paradox of mimicry also occurs, as it did in *Common Sense* and *Rights of Man*. Paine faults the patriarch Moses, the poet-prophets, the Old Testament scribes, the followers of Jesus, and the church fathers for "performances by sleight-of-hand" (1:508) when they religiously mystified natural and human matters, particularly in Scripture, in order to empower themselves politically as tyrants over others. But a close consideration of Paine's many tactics for dramatizing his own priestly authority in *The Age of Reason,* which he hopes might become (scripturally?) immortal as self-evident revelation (1:591), may also be seen as a bare performance similar to his opponents' sleight of hand. If their authority is vacant, as he asserts, then so is his own, which mimics their manner of mystifying origins whenever he uses his *religious* argument *politically* to authorize his own millennial vision of what humanity might ideally become.

While debunking miracles Paine fashions an image that we find to be remarkably reflective of this dilemma concerning authority and, as well, of Paine's self-doubt, here masked as skepticism toward others' claims to authority:

> Suppose I were to say that when I sat down to write this book a hand presented itself in the air, took up the pen and wrote every word that is herein written; would anybody believe me? Certainly they would not. Would they believe me a whit more if the thing had been a fact? Certainly they would not. (1:508)

In this passage Paine imaginatively reduces himself to a metonymic image, a mere hand. There is no body, no substantive identity behind this hand; yet it writes, and it specifically writes *this book*, the very book in the reader's hands. The author may this time have a name—Thomas Paine—but his identity is anonymous, erased in the void behind the hand. Dismembered from something empirically substantial, the identityless hand is necessarily insubstantial and unsubstantiated; yet, as if by a kind of miracle, it writes, it represents and thereby authenticates the author, who is reified and known only through the performance, the very spectacle of authorship.

What analogy could be more apt in summarizing the many conflicts informing Paine's struggle for authority in *The Age of Reason?* At the very core of this analogy lies the dilemma that Paine's literary acts of self-fathering authorship inherently incur the dismembering wound of fatherlessness; and, as Paine defined the term, to be fatherless is to be without authority. In short, self-authorization is merely an act of self-authoring, a "fictitious, and often extravagant" performance, as Paine observed of the biblical prophets. That he himself should have fashioned this image of the authoring/authorizing hand may well be a testament to his belief that "our own existence is a mystery" (1:505).

5

Paine Is
Answered

The *Age of Reason* has two histories. One concerns what Paine apparently intended to accomplish and what he actually accomplished when he wrote his book; the other concerns the way his book was read at the time of its major impact. Insofar as these readers and critics emphasized what Paine had written and the way he had written it, these two histories at times overlap; but the contemporary response to *The Age of Reason* may finally be taken as an index to the place or importance of this work well beyond Paine's own assessment of it. [1]

This second history is recorded in more than fifty pamphlets and books attacking Paine between the publication of *The Age of Reason* and the end of the century, by which time the controversy had faded. It would be tedious and fruitless to attempt a summary or an analysis of individual replies, a number of which are longer than Paine's work. Most of them were quickly and deservedly forgotten; they were relevant as argument only to the moment. Nevertheless, at least some of these same documents were avidly read when printed because of this timeliness; each was the latest installment in the controversy that many people followed, and so taken together, they tell something important. In relation to our study, these responses reveal something of late eighteenth-century attitudes toward scripture and religion as well as toward the place of religion in society and government.

In this chapter we focus on British and American responses because our research failed to discover any French controversy over *The Age of Reason*. Doubtless this silence was related to the more urgent press of revolutionary business, although French indifference toward Paine's book may be as likely an explanation. The very publication of his book in France suggests a milieu hardly resistant to its ideas, a revolutionary milieu that disestablished the church and even devised an anticlerical calendar. In this chapter, furthermore, we restrict ourselves to a description of certain features of the British and American reaction. We do not attempt, as we did with Burke and Paine, an analysis of the individual "stories" behind each of the representative voices presented here. However enticing the notion, in fact to give such a reading in each case would entail a wealth of detail that finally would amount to a series of elaborate digressions from our main subject. It is pertinent to note, in this regard, that with the exception of casual encounters with Joseph Priestley, Paine had no personal contact with the respondents included in this chapter.

Generally, the books and pamphlets of these respondents defended the literal reading of the Bible and sought to refute Paine, not on particular points of his interpretation, but rather on the principle that the Scriptures have been so long attested to and proved to be the Word of God that any doubt of or gainsaying its divinity is counter to right reason, common sense, or simple human intelligence. Accordingly, the defenders of the Bible came at Paine personally; sometimes they called him an infidel, a deist, or an atheist, but most often they addressed him as an enemy of proper thought and of the morality of decent, enlightened people.

There were three fairly well-defined opprobrious epithets used throughout this debate: *infidel, deist,* and *atheist.* They were applied with a sense of urgency and anger because of Paine's tone and style, his manner of ridicule of the Word itself, and his evident contempt for truths conventionally held sacred.

Infidel connoted an unbeliever, especially someone who either was opposed to Christianity or, while subscribing to certain of its tenets, was unfaithful to Christianity. Such a person might be abusive, or he might be quietly living a life without conventional belief. Various eighteenth-century savants, notably David Hume for one, were considered and so declared to be infidels.

Deist had a long and even distinguished lineage of definition. It was variously applied to persons professing belief in God, even God as creator of the world and final judge of mankind. But this deity was beyond the range of human experience, was certainly not equivalent to scriptural accounts, and was discovered only in the world of natural form and law as well as in the range of historical evidence as provided by the collective experience of the human race. *Deist* was variously applied in partial praise of someone who held to beliefs that were opposed to the literal reading of the Word, to belief in an immediate and vengeful deity, and to the notion of promised eternal delights in a domain so far undiscovered and unrecognized.[2]

Atheist was the most condemnatory, and the most contemporary, of the three concepts. The origins of atheism as systematic thought, and its vivid and striking appearance, can be assigned only to the later eighteenth century, not earlier when the term was used only in a very general sense. As a body of thought, atheism can be attributed to the transformation of Christian theology into a naturalism from which the Deity could easily be eliminated by way of the Universal Mathematics of René Descartes and the Universal Mechanics of Isaac Newton. By the end of the eighteenth century *atheism* had assumed a special virulence and currency. It was, some of Paine's contemporaries proclaimed, the French "poison" or "plague" that threatened to cross the Channel and fatally infect Britain. To others, this insidious incursion was more than likely; it was already evident in a steady increase of irreligion and political radicalism among the English populace.

One representative contributor to the *Gentleman's Magazine* who signed himself "R. H." resorted to scatological terms in calling Paine "a mere *scavenger* of *infidelity,* who has . . . raked all the foul kennels for every miserable offal of scepticism, to putrefy in the abominable compost of corruption with . . . his vulgar blasphemy." And in the same periodical an anonymous poetaster contributed a somewhat more moderately expressed piece of doggerel entitled "On Reading Tom Paine's *Age of Reason*":

> Tom Paines deistic trash and treason
> His impudence proclaims Right Reason,
> Or Reason's Age; but Tom should know
> He is *Right Reason*'s mad-brain'd foe;
> And that, compar'd with Sacred Writ,
> His *inch* of philosophic wit
> Is but a taper in the sun;
> Right Reason's ridicule and fun.[3]

However, of all the answers to Paine, four are particularly pertinent here.

The most formidable, and eventually the most widely circulated reply to Paine, was bishop Richard Watson's *Apology for the Bible, in a Series of Letters Addressed to Thomas Paine* (1796), which has also been printed in modern times. Watson (1737–1816) was bishop of Llandaff, a fellow of Trinity College, Cambridge, and a retired professor of divinity. At one time he had taken a progressive and liberal attitude toward dissent and reform, but in 1776, he published his *Apology for Christianity,* which was generally hailed as an answer to Edward Gibbon's "solemn sneers" in chapters 15 and 16 (on the emergence of Christianity) in the *Decline and Fall of the Roman Empire* (1776). Later, in a sermon he would expound the divine wisdom in creating an established social order comprised of rich and poor, a position assailed in William Wordsworth's *Letter to the Bishop of Llandaff,* composed about 1793. Watson was, in short, an established authority on Scripture and religion, and without realizing that his very career evidenced the precise interconnection between the clergy and the political elite condemned by Paine, he would readily raise the issue of Paine's authority.

After introductorily facing Paine with his infamous ways of denouncing Scripture, Watson undertakes to refute each of his opponent's main points in the order presented in *The Age of Reason:* the authorship of the Old Testament, the chronology of biblical events, the prophecies, and the scheme and credibility of the New Testament. Watson cogently demonstrates that Paine does not know enough; he catches Paine in several glaring mistakes, such as his comments on the collection of tithes, which Watson claims Paine owes to his sedulous aping of Voltaire. Also, concerning Paine's designation of the Decalogue as "delivered by God to Moses," Watson explains that the original Hebrew reads, Moses "began . . . to explain the law," not "Moses began to declare the law."[4]

Watson's reliance on learning, in the face of Paine's obvious and glaring ignorance, was reminiscent of Burke's earlier challenge to Paine's authority in political matters. And this maneuver doubtless made all the more impressive and perhaps devastating Watson's charges against his adversary. Watson had accordingly set the general argument for most of the more than fifty answers to *The Age of Reason*. In 1796, the year after the appearance of the second part of Paine's work, American publishers issued six printings of Watson's *Apology,* one in Albany, one in Boston, one in New Brunswick, N.J., and three in New York. One of these publishers, John Bull, reported in a preface, "Late news from England say, this work has already gone through four editions of four thousand each . . . which should prove effective in stopping the progress of deism."[5]

Gilbert Wakefield (1756–1801) countered Paine in two books, *An Examination of the Age of Reason* (1794) and *A Reply to Thomas Paine's Second Part of The Age of Reason* (1795). The immediacy of their appearance after the publication of each of Paine's two parts suggests the readiness of Wakefield's replies, which focused on two issues. First, Wakefield argued, Paine had erred in confusing the scriptural narratives with the "superstitions and fables" of the ancient world. This very linkage, Wakefield maintained, did not detract from, but proved the accuracy of Scripture by historically confirming the validity of the Old Testament and of the Gospels. In fact, the prevalent ancient Mediterranean records confirmed the accuracy of the Resurrection account.

Wakefield intermingled his religious authority with his political observations, apparently without realizing, any more than did Watson, how this procedure supported Paine's underlying contention in *The Age of Reason.* Recognizing the very strong political opposition aroused by Paine's response to Burke, Wakefield further accused his opponent of putting into jeopardy the social principles gained from the Bible and made manifest "through a succession of ages"; specifically, he condemned Paine for attempting to undermine the previous "experience" and the "present condition" of "vast aggregates of men" who have inherited and now sustain the present civilized condition of humanity.[6]

Joseph Priestley (1733–1804), English theologian and scientist, shared something of Paine's sympathy for the aims of the French Revolution, but like Watson and Wakefield, he readily mingled his expertise in religion in his discussion of political matters in, for example, his *General History of the Christian Church to the Fall of the Western Empire* (1790–1803). He had, in fact, already anticipated some of Paine's arguments against the Bible in *History of the Corruptions of Christianity* (1782) and *Lectures on History and General Policy* (1788). Especially in *Letters to a Philosophical Unbeliever* (1780, 1787), Priestley had concluded that "the truth of revelation" does not depend on the "niceties of ideas" but rather on the continuing power of the divine manifestation "to the whole human race."[7] In *An Answer to Mr. Paine's Age of Reason* (1795), designed as a continuation of *Letters*, Priestley reiterated his belief that even if the Bible were not written by divine inspiration, it nonetheless relates to the most important of all subjects, namely, the power and presence of God. Priestley also traced the rise of history from the matter of traditional symbols: images, idols, orally transmitted poems, visible monuments (such as pillars, edifices, or mere heaps of stones), coins, medals, and village or town names. This accumulation of artifacts, he concluded, demonstrates that the scriptural history is the best guide to the knowledge of "profane antiquity" because it corresponds to writings by any other ancient people. Finally, Priestley emphasized his authority on the subject: "I am much better acquainted with the Bible than Mr. Paine, and I read it daily in the original, which is certainly some advantage, and one to which Mr. Paine will not pretend."[8]

The fourth of the most cogent replies was written by David Levi (1740–99), a leading exponent of Jewish law and practice. The controversialist Levi was, by all accounts, a very considerable scholar, not only in biblical hermeneutics, but also in writings for Polish, Spanish, and Portuguese Jews. His *Defence of the Old Testament, in a Series of Letters to Thomas Paine* (1797), written in 1796, appeared in New York, not England.

In the *Defence* Levi refuted Paine on basic points of chronology and history, on the scheme and rationale of the Old Testament, and on the general tenor of the Word as having both divine and human provenience.[9] "That person, whoever he be," Levi demanded, "that attempts to criticise the scripture, ought not only to have a great knowledge of the Hebrew, but also a thorough acquaintance with the *idiom* and *phraseology* of the sacred language, so different from all others: or he will certainly fail in the attempt, and render himself ridiculous in the eyes of every discerning person, and justly merit their contempt." Levi charged Paine with being "not only a *base calumniator* but the *basest calumniator*," who had in *The Age of Reason* displayed "all the venom and vulgarity of an ignorant, impertinent, profane scoffer."[10] Levi's recurrent indictment of Paine's work was straightforward: its want of authority owing to its author's lack of pertinent learning. For Levi, Priestley, Wakefield, and Watson, Paine's strategies for claiming authority—anxious and conflicted ones, as we have seen—were utterly unsuccessful. His assertion of the sufficiency of "reason and philosophy" (1:467) in his biblical criticism was, according to his antagonists, readily refuted by various kinds of empirical evidence, especially historical and experiential.

To awaken or arouse his readers to respond to his book was doubtless one of Paine's objectives. As the rhetorical manner of *Common Sense,* the *Crisis* papers, and *Rights of Man* testifies, Paine meant for his readers to take notice of his work. If he convinced certain readers, then his voice was legitimated by their support; if he provoked other readers into opposition, then his voice was equally justified by their perverse manifestation of resistant ignorance. Even if some points made by his opponents might prevail against him, the need to mount opposition to him inherently proclaimed Paine as a force to be reckoned with.

The strategy here recalls Paine's deposing of the authority of King George III in *Common Sense* and of Burke in *Rights of Man,* which provided him with an inverse mode of self-authorization, which in turn eventually appropriated and mimicked the theatrical performance of his adversaries. The sense of urgency and the sheer force informing this body of opposition to *The Age of Reason* inadvertently subverted its overt claims of Paine's ignorance by suggesting that there was indeed something very substantial in Paine's performance that had to be fully addressed. Contrary to their design, therefore, and their scurrilous epithets notwithstanding, these replies in some sense credited Paine's voice, bestowing on its function in the debate an impression of its authority pitted against their authority (cf. 1:273). A concerted silence in response to *The Age of Reason* would indeed have been devastating to this very "authorizing" validation of Paine's voice through the process of identity by "esteemed" opposition.

Burke's previous esteemed opposition was recalled in the debate over *The Age of Reason* and informed one of the formidable established contentions special to the last decades of the eighteenth century. This contention brought Paine into contempt and odium because of his association with the French Revolution, during which he held a seat in the French National Assembly. "It should be clear," as one historian had aptly noted, "that the French revolution created the furor over Paine's pamphlet in England. Without it, the *Age of Reason* would probably have passed uncelebrated . . . to be buried alongside the earlier debate between proponents of natural and revealed religion. . . . The English establishment feared, probably overmuch, the aura of revolutionary France surrounding Paine."[11] That revolutionary aura gave rise to what was called "French infection" or what was more sensationally regarded as the "plague," the "poison" threatening England from the Continent.

Timothy Dwight (1752–1817) warned that "the present singular convulsion of Europe" had led to "the general demoralization of the human race, the depression of virtue, and the subversion of human happiness."[12] If at far-off Yale Dwight denounced this "most malignant power," in England Bishop Richard Whately (1787–1863), a prelate and university fellow, abjured the current "dangerous state of things": "About the beginning . . . of the French Revolution, it is well known that a considerable outbreak of infidelity did take place."[13]

In the 1790s this "state of things" brought forth a steady stream of sermons, public addresses, pamphlets, reports from abroad and at home, travels on the Continent, books analyzing the condition of France and its danger to both Europe and modern civilization. Collectively they described, as one contemporary anonymously averred, "a flippant, unholy, presumptuous philosophy, pretending to supply the place of Christian motives and Christian practice."[14] Still another alarmed commentator described the insidious infection spreading from the Continent to Britain as "the elegant artillery . . . of French philosophers" that was, after all, in actuality only "the smoke-balls and stink-pots" proper wholly to "English vagabonds."[15] And in a pamphlet published in 1794, another anonymous author accusingly pointed to the primary culprit:

> No man . . . has been more accessory to the enormities, murders, and miseries of wretched France, than Thomas Paine. . . . This man, whose name future generations will have cause to execrate, was driven from England to America by his crimes; he was again vomited back from

America to this country, with the contempt and abhorrence of those whom he called his friends; lastly, he was sent as a scourge to France, not daring to await here the consequence of his villainies.[16]

Sounding as if he thought the doctrine of human equality were an insidious infectious teaching, Thomas Taylor (1758–1835), a translator of Plato, asserted that Paine in particular had "convinced thousands of the equality of men to each other."[17]

Indeed, Richard Whately prophesied, the danger of this "flippant, unholy," foreign thought was not merely the implementation of "an increase of skepticism and infidelity" as a means of "attacking religion"; the greatest danger lurked in the possibility that this "infection" could spread to the "artisans and lower orders," who would likely be "for training up [as] a race of self-conceited skeptics." Whately denied that "ignorance was the best safeguard against infidelity," but he insisted that "the diffusions of increased knowledge and intellectual culture among the mass of people" were a problem because "demagogues arise, who instead of being fanatics . . . are infidels," who invite "the People . . . to judge and speak for themselves, and to assert their claims against the oppressions of priestcraft and aristocracy." With a view of the danger coming from this direction, he concluded that "the pretended 'Age of Reason' and 'Rights of Man' went hand in hand" toward a "too great diffusion of mental culture" and would hence result in "*misdirected* and *disproportionate* cultivation."[18]

The general fear recorded by Whately was effectively summarized by Burke's phrase in the *Reflections:* "a swinish multitude."[19] Burke used this expression to denote the unthinking, uncultivated masses, the irresponsible elements in society whose lack of involvement in sustaining the cultural heritage could lead them to destroy it. "Learning" would make this multitude dangerous—a notion accepted by many others who assessed the ignorant masses of otherwise devout people as persons easily swayed, even misled, by the seditious pamphlets of the infidels. [20]

In a direct assault on *The Age of Reason,* George Burges (1764?–1853), vicar of Halvergate, put the issue well: "In the present crisis, when every venerable institution is tottering to its base, and every bond of society is in danger of being dissevered, it is impossible to calculate the mischievous effects, which the eradication of Christianity would produce in society. . . . By weakening the credibility of the religion of the multitude, you weaken the strongest check upon immorality."[21] Irreligion threatened, these spokesmen claimed, the majority of citizens, whose intelligence was incapable of reasoning and whose emotions and prejudices could be easily managed as massive instruments of destruction to society and to the state.

These would-be guardians of the ignorant masses indeed perceived something; for, as we saw in chapter 4, in *The Age of Reason* Paine's offensive against Scripture was really a campaign against authority, the established monarchical and aristocratic hegemony reinforced by scripture and religion. For him the present political apparatus was little more than a monarchical administrative machine, a system of government engineered through a superstitious tribute to an outmoded religion, itself founded on a long-dead and bogus scriptural authority. Paine saw plainly that social power had been appropriated entirely by political and religious leaders, who conspired together to keep this power from the people, to whom it properly belonged by the laws of nature and reason. He believed that this pattern had roots in antiquity, when kings and priests pretended to be saviors with control over life and fertility, over nature itself; and he accordingly associated the theory of the divine right of the monarchs of his day with this primitive notion in remote antiquity of the relationship between the rule of the deity and the rule of the king and the priest.[22]

Sensing, if not quite delineating, this larger agenda in *The Age of Reason,* Paine's detractors worried about the effect of his book on the masses. Paine's assault on Scripture had profound social implications; for it put at risk a seemingly incontestable and virtually inarticulable principle: that a biblically based Christianity alone was the foundation, the strength, and the maintenance of civilized, modern Western society. Without biblical prescriptions devotedly, even unquestioningly, adhered to by the masses, the rule of law and government, Western civilization itself as a way of life, was unthinkable. Paine's opponents sensed in their bones that the harmony or alliance between religion and civil policy was, as Dwight had proclaimed, indispensable for human happiness.

These sentiments especially informed the English *Weltanschauung.* As one of Paine's British contemporaries declared to a university audience, the influence of the Bible on humanity had exerted a great moral effect in England, where there exists more pure and apostolic character than in revolutionary and atheistic France, or in any other country. And, he concluded, even though the purity of this revelation has been somewhat countered by corrupt manners and false philosophy at the end of the century, nevertheless, the principles of God's truth remained strong in the English national character.[23] English citizens, educated and uneducated alike, generally at that time took for granted that divine providence operated effectively to direct their government. It was a government that in the exercise of its power had always mingled religion and politics.

So Paine sought to undermine Scripture in order to subvert Christianity in order to overthrow the prevalent hierarchical political structures of

England and the rest of Europe. When his detractors declaimed with intense alarm about the societal implications—the effect on the masses—of Paine's move against Scripture, they rightly sensed that his great crime was indeed his contempt and vilification of the political and social establishment. He had not only deposed the power elite of kings, aristocrats, and priests, but he had also assailed the very religio-political ground of, the "reason" behind, the "authority" of Western culture at the end of the eighteenth century.

Conclusion: "I Can Write
a Better Book Myself"

In the earlier chapters we detailed the intellectual context and the personal pretext of *The Age of Reason,* both of which concerns reinforce one recent historian's contention that "religion just as much as politics is concerned with power."[1] In this chapter we take up a somewhat related matter by briefly suggesting several ways that Paine's political book participates in the tradition of spiritual relation, conversion narrative, or confession in early America. Although a comparison of Paine's work with the Quaker tradition of confession, typified by John Woolman's *Journal,* is especially pertinent, his book can also be approached in terms of two general features found in the Puritan tradition of confession.

Perhaps the central moment of Paine's conversion, at least as reported in *The Age of Reason*, occurred when he was "seven or eight years of age" while he listened to "a sermon read by a relation of [his], who was a great devotee of the Church, upon the subject of what was called *redemption by the death of the Son of God."* Paine "revolted at . . . what [he] had heard, and thought to [himself] that it was making God Almighty act like a passionate man who killed His son when He could not revenge Himself in any other way." Late in life, Paine emphasized the pivotal importance of this episode to him, and in our Introduction we similarly indicated how this resistance to all manner of filiacide became the vital heart of his career. Paine insisted that "this was not one of that kind of thoughts that had anything in it of childish levity"; in contrast to mere temporary youthful insubordination, his insight "was to [him] a serious reflection" that he "believe[d] in the same manner" later in life (1:497).

Paine highlights the importance of this event by situating it dramatically in a memorable physical setting, which the reader is invited to visualize even as the author "perfectly recollect[s] the spot." Paine's "serious reflection" occurred after he entered a garden, specifically "as [he] was going down the garden steps" (1:497). Any evocation here of the famous garden scene in that classic conversion narrative, Augustine's *Confessions,* may be entirely accidental. Nevertheless, the image of the garden itself is not likely presented here casually; for garden imagery figures throughout Paine's early writings whenever, as we remarked in the Introduction, he speaks Miltonically of the human paradise lost to Satanic monarchical forces. And a revisionary notion of paradise regained informs his millennial vision of what humanity, emancipated from the despotism of these regal forces, can accomplish on earth—a secular humanism reinforced by the Quaker belief that individuals can, through the workings of the Inward Light, break free from corruption and achieve perfection while on earth.[2]

But this belief notwithstanding, Quaker dogma was, in Paine's opinion, itself inadequate for the recovery of this garden of human possibility: "If the taste of a Quaker could have been consulted at the Creation . . . not a flower would have blossomed its gayeties, nor a bird been permitted to sing" (1:498). Rejecting the traditional religious notion of heavenly ascent out of paradise lost, Paine *descends* the garden steps to this scene of conversion. In this action one may glimpse a metaphoric harbinger of his manner in *The Age of Reason:* a confession of his loss of conventional religious belief that sometimes inverts and sometimes recuperates in decidedly "descendant" political (secular) terms the authoritative tradition of the spiritual relation.

Paine's book shares with traditional early American Quaker conversion narratives an introductory statement of purpose, a fervid sense of inward inspiration, a declared expression of conscience, and an evangelical intention to instruct others. [3] In contrast, however, Paine reverses the usual confessional objective in quoting Scripture and violates the usual style of restraint characteristic of Quaker spiritual relations. Although he does not conform to the Woolman model of diminishing the self in transparent prose, he does variously equivocate (as we noted throughout our study) the autonomy of his voice in a style designed (he thought) to reveal the universal and to appeal to common human reason. In this sense, *The Age of Reason* mirrors, whether by authorial accident or intention, the tension between the subjective personal and the universal impersonal that occurs in early American spiritual autobiographies.

In claiming to speak of the universal (the rights of man) through the intellect (common sense), Paine represents himself as a typical person—a characteristic pose in spiritual relations[4]—not only in what humanity has collectively shared in the current age of fable and superstition, but also in what it may collectively become in a millennial age of reason. As we observed in the Introduction apropos the issue of authority, this dual voice produces various tensions. In terms of the genre of spiritual relation, he seems, on the one hand, to address the world of ordinary manners and comfortable relationships, where he and his readers share a certain intimacy with Scripture and the systems of belief founded on it; this feature suggests that his conversion narrative can be trusted because his authority derives *externally* from the commonplace experiences that his readers already know and confirm. On the other hand, as a "new man," he seems to address a different world, yet to be born, where the ordinary manners and comfortable relationships of the past would be transformed into something transcending commonplace experience. This latter feature suggests that his conversion narrative can be trusted because his authority derives *internally* from the honest examination of his conscience, illuminated (as it were) by an Inward Light. Both voices merge in Paine's enumeration of proofs, as he traces his progress from early acceptance of conventional *religious* belief toward a counterconversion to a more enlightened *political* faith, which he had earlier described as a "counter-revolution" (1:356).

Paine's contemporary reader, in other words, encountered in *The Age of Reason* the customary resonance of the Bible as it sounded to a memory intimately versed in Scripture and, as well, the heretical polemic of the narrator as he provided a parallel commentary insisting on rereading Scripture in a quite unusual way. The latter voice seemed more prevalent to these readers because Paine's goal was to convert them, and as one means to this end he fashioned a language and argument differing from what was normal or expected. This language was intended to startle, even shock, if it was to awaken the potential citizens of paradise regained. Thus, in rejecting the dogma of the past, the dogma of church and state founded on Scripture, Paine violated the conventional restraint customarily featured in discussions of Scripture. He accomplished this revision by incorporating elements of two other genres within his modified conversion narrative: one, a journalistic approach to the average person; the other, a biblical-commentary approach to the educated person.

Of Paine's two imagined audiences, the middle-class laborers usually did not pursue the heady reaches of Burkean debate, whereas these readers did seek out the sensational and satiric exposés of journalism. In *The Age of Reason*, as throughout his career, Paine accommodated their taste. To speak of Moses as a "wretch," as "among the detestable villains that in any period of the world have disgraced the name of man," was as scandalously distasteful and sensationally provocative as his characterization of Solomon as "a worn-out debauchee" (1:528, 550); and these instances are but two examples in a book replete with similar abusive labeling.[5] In this way the disrespectful and irreverent "Pain," as his critics dubbed him, not only appropriated the genre of the spiritual confession to assail Holy Writ, but he also managed certain common journalistic features—such as anecdote, irony, parody, satire, feigned confusion, folk matter, concrete vocabulary, and appeals to authority at one point and to common sense at another, among other devices—to attract the readers he most sought to convert to his political beliefs.

Besides rhetorical strategies derived from journalism, Paine also confiscated a technique of biblical commentary used prevalently since the Reformation to bring the scriptural doctrines to educated people's attention: statement, reasons, and conclusion. In contrast to relying on the usual historical pattern and scholarly manner in applying this tripartite scheme, Paine adapted it to subject Holy Writ to certain present-day tests of experiential or empirical validity. Aside from the longstanding argument that the Bible is a timeless work, Paine's certainty that the Word actually evidenced a latter-day form and order encouraged him to subject Scripture to the empirical tests of his day. There was, as well, the fact of the centuries-long history of theological debate about Scripture—indeed, (from his point of view) the manifest disputation between the biblical passages themselves—to encourage further his own present contention with Holy Writ. In applying his present-day tests of "reason," Paine found the Bible to be a book so "manifestly obscure, disorderly, and contradictory" that he could not "believe" it to be the Deity's "work"; "I can write a better book myself," (2:737), he brazenly declared in a Paris pamphlet in 1797. Paine, in short, approached the Bible as a conflicted text to be analyzed in the same way as any document of his day, just as his own scripture-like spiritual relation in *The Age of Reason* might be analyzed for its underlying political contentiousness.

In this way, Paine descended the garden stairs in still another metaphoric sense. He traced through Scripture a contradictory movement reversing the one typical of the scheme of biblical commentary. The persons and events in the Bible could, he argued, be properly described by demoting them from the ingratiatingly sacred to the derisively human and profane. He even imitated and parodied certain patterns of scriptural exegesis by biblical authorities: paraphrases of the divine Word in modern terms, elaborations of gnomish utterances into grand abstractions, and demarcations of intricate linkages between various parts of Holy Writ.

Whether appropriating a journalistic mode of discourse for the average reader or inverting a biblical-commentary mode of discourse for the educated reader, Paine vacillated in tone between seriousness and jocularity— the mark of many an eighteenth-century satirist. His virtual scandal of aggressive and outrageous utterance particularly attracted the attention of his adversaries, who were incensed by his persona of the jesting polemicist. Enraging these adversaries, however, was doubtless a part of his intent; for he expressed no surprise, no distress, over their subsequent vilification of him. That very defamation or notoriety inadvertently granted his own voice credibility and substance through its esteemed opposition (as we noted throughout our study) and, at the same time, brought into the open before the mass of humanity critical issues that heretofore had, by and large, been the assumed purview of the self-appointed, despotic guardians of humanity.

And Paine could count on the curiosity of this middle-class audience to work for him, too. That "figuring" audience, newly emerged with the rise of newspapers,[6] would likely be provoked emotionally by imagining what might happen as a result of Paine's book if its viewpoint came to pass—became canonical—and if the Bible and the Christian church were indeed overthrown. In other words, Paine doubtless anticipated how this potential curious audience would "build images" at every moment of its reading of his book, how it would create (in a combination of wonder and fear) imagined possibilities as it pursued the author's imaginative "plot" against the Deity, the church, and (if it sensed his underlying agenda) even the constitutional government. Converting this audience of popular readers, even more than his audience of educated readers, to his "inspired" political insight—the need to depose all patriarchal forces to prevent the continuation of generational filiacide and to regain paradise on earth—was the goal of Paine's *Age of Reason,* a spiritual relation with a counter-religious design declared by a voice performing between personal autonomy and impersonal authority.

As we observed throughout the preceding chapters, Paine mediates the various paradoxes of his quest for authority through this performance of voice. Pertinently, in the American tradition of the spiritual relation the prescriptive use of language, textual expression, tends to create the character of the confessor.[7] In our view, however, Paine never quite creates himself in any definitive sense in his conversion narrative. His identity, ever negotiating its authority through a linguistic performance of opposition, is necessarily left as incomplete as is the paratactic *The Age of Reason* as an argument and as a text.

To stop writing, to stop the theatrical spectacle of his performance, would in some profound sense be the loss of its author's identity and authority. It is not at all surprising, therefore, that the second part to *The Age of Reason* was followed by a third in the last years of his life. For this undertaking, he informed himself even more carefully than previously in specific details on the relation between Old Testament prophecies and New Testament fulfillment. He learned much more about the possible derivation of the Israelite religion and certain ecclesiastical practices from the Persians and other Eastern neighbors. He acquired further information on the history of the early Christian church and the first councils, especially on the likelihood of editorial tampering with the Word in the centuries before the Reformation.

Paine wanted to publish his more current findings as part 3 of *The Age of Reason*. His manuscript, entitled *Examination of the Prophecies,* specifically treated the connection between the Old Testament prophecies and the coming of the Messiah in the New Testament (2:848–92). This tract was certainly ready by 1802, but Jefferson dissuaded Paine from publishing it lest it get a vitriolic reception, or worse. Nevertheless, it appeared in 1807 as *An Examination of the Passages in the New Testament, Quoted from the Old and Called Prophecies Concerning Jesus Christ.* It was Paine's last published work.

Paine could not quit, and in the main, all that he wrote after 1795 was an addendum to his *apologia* (at once a defense and an apology) entitled *The Age of Reason*. Paine was the book, and the book was Paine, as his image of the dismembered writing hand implied (chapter 4). Sleight of hand characterized the confession of one in the other; for confession is a system of representation and exchange, in which everything seems orderly and fixed, whereas nothing is eventually what it seems to be.[8] Simultaneously a defense of and an abdication of authority, confession presents causes to explain effects that finally elude those very causal explanations. In short, Paine's identity remained a process, his authenticity and authority realized through the authorial performance of opposing voice. His work, his identity, was no more finally consummated than was, in his view, *The Age of Reason* as a book or the millennial age of reason heralded in that book.

A number of early American Puritan conversion narratives reveal a similar lack of completion in structure and resolution.[9] That *The Age of Reason,* as Paine's spiritual relation, evinces a similar pattern is less the result of any influence by these prior documents than it is the effect of the unsettled nature of the early Republic[10] as well as of Paine's own restless nature. Nevertheless, the similarity is worth observing because, whether by authorial design or accident, the lack of finish in *The Age of Reason* becomes an apt narrative strategy in Paine's effort to convert others to his antibiblical, political humanism.

Conversion requires the falling away of old views so that new perceptions can be born into the world. Violence toward the dying age of fable and superstition is inherent in Paine's apparently inappropriate application of "coarse" journalistic strategies in discussing Scripture, in his employment of virtually scandalous language, in his reversal of the argumentative schemata of biblical commentary, in his creation of the persona of a jesting polemicist, and in his revision of the spiritual relation. This assault on the bulwark of convention and tradition elicits curiosity and engenders some confusion in the reader. This confusion presumably amounts to a crack in the defensive religio-political wall stormed by Paine, and it is potentially a prelude to skepticism and doubt. Paine evidently held a view similar to the Goethean proverb, "Doubt grows with knowledge." And doubt, Paine knew well from his scriptural studies, is inimical to religious faith, as Jesus indicated clearly (Matt. 21:21; Mark 11:23). Paul was even more direct: "He that doubteth is damned" (Rom. 14:23).

The somewhat disheveled manner and unfinished nature of Paine's spiritual relation in *The Age of Reason* represent more than the inevitable consequence of the kind of book he was writing. To some extent, of course, these features do indeed suggest the process of intellectual growth, a process that would not be completed until Paine's death.[11] But these same features also represent his always incomplete and unconsummated identity, its authenticity and authority validated only through its anxious authorial performance.

And these same two features also serve, perhaps only by happenstance, as an apt heuristic urging Paine's readers to continue a similar religious reformation and political revolution within themselves. In a sense, his example instructs his readers to engage in a processive revisionism within themselves and in their world. Paine's confession exhorts his readers to "write a better book" through their realization of heretofore repressed human potentialities. His spiritual relation in effect exhorts his readers to give, in their thoughts and in their actions, a *scriptural testimony,* as it were, of the latent capacities of the human mind and society, capacities far beyond anything suggested in the Bible, especially as used by church and state in the subjugation of humanity throughout history. For Paine, the descent of the garden steps (by means of *dissent)* to the interior of the mind implies that a discredited external authority can be inverted and that a credited internal autonomy can be asserted in its stead. Descending the garden steps to the interior of the dissenting mind creates the possibility of conversion, or the transformation of outmoded *religious* beliefs into a *political* paradise regained.

Appendix 1:
The Composition of
The Age of Reason

Late in 1793, Paine was the most prominent among a group of expatriate radicals resident in Paris who in those heady months met to talk and plan in the great mansion that had once housed Madame de Pompadour. [1] It was there, so reports then and afterward suggested, that Paine set down a version of his articles of religious belief that, as he wrote Samuel Adams, might *"renovate the age"* and prevent "the people of France [from] running headlong into atheism." To that end Paine stated, "This is exactly my religion, and the whole of it. . . . *I believe in God.*"[2]

Paine had left no record or hint of the stages, if there were any, of the writing of the first part of *The Age of Reason.* Knowing his facility in quick composition both in his American years and in his controversy with Burke, we can well assume that he wrote a draft within a short time during the late autumn or early winter of 1793. He later stated that he had written that "former part" before he was imprisoned, and he "congratulated" himself on so doing (1:516). "When I wrote the former part," he further stressed, "I had neither Bible nor Testament to refer to, nor could I procure any. My own situation, even as to existence, was becoming every day more precarious, and . . . I was obliged to be quick and concise" (1:582). Indeed, in Paine's account of events, he had finished writing the last pages only "six hours" before he was taken to the Luxembourg prison, and his American friend Joel Barlow was left with the task of seeing the manuscript into print.[3]

After a life-threatening stay of ten months and nine days, Paine was released from prison in November 1794 and then recovered his health at the residence of James Monroe, who had secured Paine's release. There, with a Bible for reference, he wrote the longer and closely argued second part of *The Age of Reason.* Paine's point of view in this part suggests that he has come through some difficulty registered in the first part and is now free to express himself as frankly and cogently as he can. Whatever the full explanation for this modification of point of view, one factor may have been that he now had at hand the evidence, the Bible itself, to support what he had written earlier and was reinforcing now. There is, he must have felt, a difference in depending on memory and on the text itself.

The first edition of *The Age of Reason* is, as one commentator has noted, "a bibliographical enigma."[4] Some authorities give the date 1793 for the first edition, and it has been suggested that the earliest publication bearing the date of 1793 was suppressed. Yet in a letter to Samuel Adams, Paine stated that he had authorized a translation of the book (that is, what would later be the first part) into French to "stay the progress of atheism," his opposition to which had endangered his life;[5] and J. M. Querard's bibliography of French literature indeed gives 1793 as the date of the first edition of *L'age de la raison*.

Paine is said to have subsidized the publication of his book.[6] It was published, in English at least, in March 1794 by Joel Barlow in England while Paine was in prison in France. This printing sold for a mere three pence, cheap enough for the work to circulate among many ordinary readers and to arouse the ire of its opponents , who felt the need to counter its seditious effects.

The second part of *The Age of Reason* was published in October 1795. Paine ordered fifteen thousand copies for the American market alone and underwrote the publication himself. It was first sold, however, in London in that year in a pirated edition of H. D. Symonds and had a limited circulation. When Paine discovered that Symonds had surreptitiously printed his work, he forwarded an authentic manuscript of part 2 to Daniel Eaton in London and instructed him to print a cheap edition. This work, combining both parts, appeared in 1796, and sold for one shilling, sixpence.[7]

Francis Place also arranged an edition of both parts in 1796, with the help of the bookseller Thomas Williams; it sold two thousand copies in that year. Williams then produced another, larger printing, but before he could sell all the copies priced at one shilling, the British government indicted him, suppressed the pamphlet, and began to confiscate copies. Thus, between March 1794 and the decision to suppress both parts at the end of 1796, only a few editions of *The Age of Reason* came before the public. The book was not republished in England until 1818, when Richard Carlile produced an edition of Paine's *Theological Works*.

There was no limitation on or suppression of Paine's book in the United States; however, to please people who did not approve of Paine's theological treatise and wished to read his writings without it, some American printings omitted *The Age of Reason* entirely. And to accommodate still other people who wished to read both sides of the issue, some sets were bound up with Bishop Richard Watson's *Apology for the Bible,* in "Carey's Third Philadelphia Edition"; Watson's reply to Paine, discussed in chapter 5, was the most popular and widely circulated response of the many replies that were printed in the years immediately following the publication of the complete *Age of Reason.* The Library of Congress copy of the 1797 edition of Paine's *Works* contains such an addition of Watson's *Apology,* although curiously *The Age of Reason,* which is listed at the end of the table of contents of the second volume, does not in fact appear in that copy.[8]

In 1797, James Carey, a Philadelphia publisher, brought out a two-volume edition of Paine's collected writings containing all his extant works. *The Age of Reason* occupied the final pages of the second volume of this edition. In the first volume the advertisement from the editor contained a cautionary statement: "Several subscribers, and others, expressing a wish to have THE AGE OF REASON omitted in their volumes, the work has been printed so as to accommodate them: —to this end it was necessary to print that treatise distinctly from the body of the work, so that it may be bound up at the end of the [second] volume or wholly omitted."[9] In most printings of the two-volume edition, *The Age of Reason* was placed at the end of the second volume and was paginated separately. In after years to the present, there have been almost innumerable printings of what is, in our opinion, Paine's most noteworthy book.

Appendix 2:
A Representative Alphabetical List
of Contemporary Responses to
The Age of Reason (1794–98)

Works consulted, in our failed effort to locate French responses to *The Age of Reason,* included, among other comprehensive bibliographies, André Monglond's *La France révolutionaire et impériale* (1930–63); André Martin and Gérard Walter's *Catalogue de l'histoire de la Révolution Française* (1936–69); and George R. Haven and Donald F. Bond's *A Cultural Bibliography of French Literature, Vol. 4: The Eighteenth Century* (1951).

The New Annual Register is divided into three sections, each section with separate and independent pagination beginning with page 1. The first section contains simple, unmarked pagination; the second has page numbers enclosed in parentheses; the third, containing reviews, encloses the numbers in square brackets.

Entries marked by an asterisk (*) depend on listings in *Literary Reviews in British Periodicals, 1789–1797: A Bibliography,* compiled by William S. Ward (New York: Garland, 1979), pp. 289–311.

Political cartoons responding to Paine are not included here. A few of them are identified in Mary Dorothy George's *Catalogue of Political and Personal Satires, Vol. 7: 1743–1800* (London: British Museum, 1942).

Anonymous. *The Age of Confusion taken for that of Reason, by Mr. Paine: or, a Defence of the Christian Religion against the Attacks of this Thomas, containing an Abridgement of the Proofs which determine all Reasonable Men to Acknowledge Jesus Christ as the Promised Messiah. By a Layman.* London, 1794.

Analytical Review. 20 (November 1794): 287–88.

———. *The Age of Disorder Mistaken by Mr. Paine for the Age of Reason; or, a Defense of the Christian Religion against the Attacks of this Thomas; containing a Summary of the Proofs which induce all Reasonable Persons to acknowledge Jesus Christ for the Messiah foretold by the Prophets. By a Layman.* London, 1797.

Critical Review. Ser. 2. 21 (December 1797): 345.

Monthly Review. N.s. 15 (December 1797): 463.

———. *Christianity the Only True Theology; or, an Answer to Mr. Paine's "Age of Reason." By a Churchman.* London, 1794.

Analytical Review. 20 (November 1794): 285–87.

Anthologica Hibernica. 4 (1794): 366.*

Critical Review. Ser. 2. 13 (March 1795): 348–50.

English Review. 25 (January 1795): 140.

———. *Deism Disarmed[;] or, a short Answer to Paine's "Age of Reason," on Principles Self-Evident but Seldom Produced.* London, 1794.

Analytical Review. 20 (December 1794): 402–3.

Critical Review. Ser. 2 13 (March 1795): 347–48.

English Review. 25 (January 1795): 140.

Monthly Review. N.s. 15 (December 1795): 462–63.

New Annual Register. 15 (1794): [178].

Scots Magazine. 56 (Appendix, 1794): 838.

———. *A Discourse occasioned by the Death of Alexander Christie . . . Containing some Observations on the Progress of Religious Knowledge in Scotland, and on Mr. Paine's "Age of Reason." By a Layman.* Glasgow and London, 1795.

Analytical Review. 22 (July 1795): 71.

Critical Review. Ser. 2. 16 (February 1796): 227.

English Review. 27 (February 1796): 187–88.

———. *A Letter to the Analytical Reviewers; Being an Examination of their Account of the "Age of Reason" . . . by Thomas Paine. To which is added, an Address to the People of England. By a True Briton, and a Graduate of an English University.* London and Southampton, 1794.

Analytical Review. 20 (December 1794): 484–85.

Critical Review. Ser 2. 14 (June 1795): 236.

———. *Pastoral Letters to the Youth of a Congregation: in Answer to Mr. Paine's "Age of Reason."* London, 1795.

Protestant Dissenter's Magazine. 2 (1795): 26–27, 67–69, 148–50, 236–38.*

———. *Remarks on a Pamphlet Entitled the "Age of Reason," being an Investigation of True and Fabulous Theology, by Thomas Paine. By a Protestant Lay-Dissenter.* Dublin, 1795.

Analytical Review. 22 (July 1795): 194.

Monthly Review. N.s. 18 (November 1795): 352.

New Annual Register. 18 (1795): [198].

————. *Thomas Paine Vindicated; being a Short Letter to the Bishop of Llandaff's Reply to Thomas Paine's "Age of Reason." By a Deist.* London, 1796.

British Critic. 9 (April 1797): 449.

Critical Review. Ser. 2. 20 (July 1797): 349.

Monthly Review. N.s. 21 (September 1796): 105.

————. *Three Letters. Addressed to the Readers of Paine's "Age of Reason." By one of the People called Christian.* London, 1797.

British Critic. 9 (April 1797): 449.

Critical Review. Ser. 2. 21 (December 1797): 468.

Auchincloss, J. *The Sophistry of the first Part of Mr. Paine's "Age of Reason." Or a Rational Vindication of the Holy Scriptures as a Positive Revelation from God: with the Causes of Deism. In three Sermons.* Stockport and London, 1796.

Analytical Review. 23 (March 1796): 263–64.

British Critic. 8 (July 1796): 427.

Evangelical Magazine. 4 (1796): 392–93.*

Monthly Review. N.s. 20 (May 1796): 102–3.

New Annual Register. 17 (1796): [186].

————. *The Sophistry of Both the First and Second Part of Mr. Paine's "Age of Reason"; or a Rational Vindication of the Holy Scriptures as a Positive Revelation from God, with the Causes of Deism in four Sermons.* Edinburgh, 1796.

Belknap, Jeremy. *Dissertations on the Character, Death, & Resurrection of Jesus Christ, and the Evidence of the Gospel; with Remarks on . . . a book Intitled "The Age of Reason."* Boston, 1795.

Benjoin, George. *The Integrity and Excellence of Scripture. A Vindication of the Much-Controverted Passages, Deut. vii. 2.5 and xx. 16, 17. Whereby the Justness of the Commands they enjoin are incontrovertibly Proved, and Consequentially, the Objections of Thomas Paine and Dr. Geddes compleately Refuted.* London, 1797.

Critical Review. Ser. 2. 23 (July 1798): 340.

Gentleman's Magazine. 68 (February 1798): 135–36.

Bentley, Thomas. *Reason and Revelation; or a Brief Answer to Thomas Paine's Late Work, Entitled "The Age of Reason."* London, 1794.

Analytical Review. 19 (August 1794): 478.

New Annual Register. 17 (1796): [186].

Binns, Abraham. *Remarks on a Publication, Entitled "A Serious Admonition to the Disciples of Thomas Paine, and All Other Infidels."* London, 1796.

Analytical Review. 25 (February 1797): 302.

Critical Review. Ser. 2. 20 (May 1797): 109.

Bousell, John. *The Ram's Horn Sounded Seven Times. . . . also Remarks upon T. Paine's Second Part of "The Age of Reason."* Norwich, 1799.

Burges, George. *A Letter to Thomas Paine, Author of "The Age of Reason."* Peterborough and London, 1795.

Analytical Review. 21 (March 1795): 304–5.

British Critic. 6 (December 1795): 675–76.

Monthly Review. N.s. 16 (April 1795): 458–59.

Chip, Will (Hannah More, pseud.). *A Country Carpenter's Confession of Faith; with a few plain Remarks on "The Age of Reason."* London, 1794.

London Chronicle. 12 November 1794, p. 468.

[Cobbett, William.] *An Antidote for Tom Paine's Theological and Political Poison.* Philadelphia, 1796.

Coward, John. *Deism Traced to One of Its Principal Sources, or the Corruption of Christianity by the Grand Cause of Infidelity . . . In Answer to Mr. Paine's Second Part of the "Age of Reason."* London, 1796.

British Critic. 9 (February 1797): 200.

Critical Review. Ser. 2. 22 (February 1798): 222–23.

Monthly Review. N.s. 21 (September 1796): 104–5.

Dutton, Thomas. *A Vindication of "The Age of Reason," by Thomas Paine: in Answer to the Strictures of Mr. Gilbert Wakefield, and Dr. Priestley, on this Celebrated Performance.* London, 1795.

Analytical Review. 23 (January 1796): 56–57.

British Critic. 7 (March 1796): 327.

Critical Review. Ser. 2. 16 (April 1796): 401–5.

English Review. 26 (December 1795): 456–57.

Monthly Review. N.s. 19 (January 1796): 165.

New Annual Review. 16 (1795): [198].

Estlin, John Prior. *Evidences of Revealed Religion, and Particularly Christianity, Stated with Reference to a Pamphlet called "The Age of Reason."* Bristol and London, 1795.

Analytical Review. 23 (April 1796): 405–10.

Critical Review. Ser. 2. 19 (January 1797): 229–30.

English Review. 27 (April 1796): 475.

[Fisher, Meirs.] *A Reply to the False Reasoning of "The Age of Reason." By a Layman.* Philadelphia, 1796.

Helton, John. *The Insufficiency of the Light of Nature: Exemplified in the Vices and Depravity of the Heathen World. Including some Strictures on Paine's "Age of Reason."* London, 1797.

Analytical Review. 26 (November 1797): 573.

European Magazine. 32 (December 1797): 400.

Hincks, Thomas Dix. *Letters Originally Addressed to the Inhabitants of Cork. In Defense of Revealed Religion, Occasioned by the Circulation of a Work Entitled "The Age of Reason" in that City.* Bristol, 1796.

Analytical Review. 24 (July 1796): 69–70

British Critic. 9 (April 1797): 437.

New Annual Register. 16 (1795): [198.]

[Humphreys, Daniel.] *The Bible Needs No Apology . . . A Short Answer to Paine: in Four Letters, on Watson's "Apology for the Bible" and Paine's "Age of Reason,"* Part the Second. Portsmouth, N.H., 1796.

Jackson, William. *Observations in Answer to Mr. Thomas Paine's "Age of Reason."* London, 1795.

Analytical Review. 22 (July 1795): 66–68.

British Critic. 7 (May 1796): 557–58.

British Magazine. 65 (September 1795): 758–59.

Critical Review. Ser. 2 19 (February 1797): 227–29.

Gentleman's Magazine. 65 (September 1795): 758–59.

Monthly Review. N.s. 17 (May 1795): 219.

New Annual Register. 16 (1795): [197–98].

Levi, David. *Defence of the Old Testament, in a Series of Letters Addressed to Thomas Paine.* New York, 1797.

M'Neilie, Daniel. *Dogmatism Exposed, and Sophistry Detected: or, a Confutation of Paine's "Age of Reason." To which is Prefixed, a Brief Account of the Replies Already published.* London, 1794.

Analytical Review. 20 (December 1794): 401–2.

British Critic. 5 (January 1795): 76.

Critical Review. Ser. 2. 12 (December 1794): 470.

English Review. 25 (January 1795): 140.

Monthly Review. N.s. 16 (January 1795): 217–18.

New Annual Register. 15 (1794): [178–79].

Malham, John. *A Word for the Bible: being a Serious Reply . . . to the Speculative Deists and Practical Atheists of Modern Times: particularly "The Age of Reason," Part the Second, by Thomas Paine.* London, 1796.

Analytical Review. 23 (April 1796): 403–5.

British Critic. 8 (October 1796): 426.

English Review. 27 (April 1796): 263.

Gentleman's Magazine. 66 (October 1796): 859.

Monthly Review. N.s. 20 (May 1796): 103.

Martin, John. *A Letter to the Honourable Thomas Erskine, with a Postscript to the Right Honourable Lord Kenyon, upon their Conduct at the Trial of*

Thomas Paine, for Publishing Paine's "Age of Reason." London, 1797.

Critical Review. Ser. 2. 21 (December 1797): 478.

Meek, T. *Sophistry Detected; or a Refutation of T. Paine's "Age of Reason."* London, 1795.

Evangelical Magazine. 3 (1795): 472–73.*

Muir, James. *An Examination of the Principles Contained in "The Age of Reason." In Ten Discourses.* Baltimore, 1795.

Nash, Michael. *Paine's "Age of Reason" Measured by the Standard of Truth: Wakefield's Examination of, and a Layman's Answer to . . . "The Age of Reason," both Weighed in the Balance, and found Wanting.* London, 1794.

Analytical Review. 20 (October 1794): 202–3.

British Critic. 6 (September 1795): 323.

Critical Review. Ser. 2. 14 (August 1795): 459–60.

Evangelical Magazine. 3 (1795): 298.*

Literary Review and Historical Journal. 1 (1794): 273–75.*

Monthly Review. N.s. 15 (October 1794): 342–43.

New Annual Register. 15 (1794): [179].

Ogden, Uzal. *Antidote to Deism. The Deist Unmasked; or an Ample Refutation of All the Objections to T. Paine as contained in a Pamphlet intitled "The Age of Reason."* Newark, N.J., 1795.

Osborn, J. *Scripture and Reason, a Poem Containing . . . Arguments in Refutation of Mr. Paine's "Age of Reason."* London, 1795.

Padman, J., Jr. *A Layman's Protest against the Profane Blasphemy, False Charges, and Illiberal Invective of Thomas Paine, Author of a Book, Entitled "The Age of Reason." Part I and II, being an Investigation of True and fabulous Theology.* London, 1797.

Critical Review. Ser. 2. 20 (August 1797): 466.

European Magazine. 32 (July 1797): 34.

Gentleman's Magazine. 68 (July 1798): 603–4.

New Annual Register. 18 (1797): [207].

Palmer, Elihu. *The Examiners Examined: Being a Defense of "The Age of Reason."* New York, 1794.

Patten, William. *Christianity the True Theology and only Perfect Moral System, in Answer to "The Age of Reason."* Warren, R.I., 1795.

Priestley, Joseph. *An Answer to Mr. Paine's "Age of Reason," Being a Continuation of Letters to the Philosophers and Politicians of France, on the Subject of Religion; and the Letters to a Philosophical Unbeliever. With a Preface by Theophilus Lindsey.* London, 1795.

Analytical Review. 21 (June 1795): 630–36.

British Critic. 6 (July 1795): 174–78.

English Review. 27 (April 1796): 260–62.

New Annual Register. 16 (1795): [197].

Protestant Dissenter's Magazine. 2 (1795): 349–50.*

Scots Magazine. 57 (August 1795)): 512.

———. *Letters to a Philosophical Unbeliever. Part III. Containing an Answer to Mr. Paine's "Age of Reason." The Second Edition.* Philadelphia, 1795.

Scott, Thomas. *A Vindication of the Divine Inspiration of the Holy Scriptures, and of the Doctrines Contained in Them; Being an Answer to the two parts of Mr. T. Paine's "Age of Reason."* London, 1796.

Analytical Review. 25 (January 1797): 60–62.

Critical Review. Ser. 2. 20 (May 1797): 106–8.

Taylor, Thomas. *An Answer to the First Part of "The Age of Reason."* Manchester, 1796.

———. *A Vindication of the Rights of Brutes.* Boston, 1795.

Thomas, Robert. *The Cause of Truth; Containing . . . a Refutation of Errors in the Political Works of Thomas Paine, and Other Publications of a Similar Kind; in a Series of Letters of a Religious, Moral, and Political Nature.* London, 1798.

European Magazine. 32 (December 1797): 400.

Gentleman's Magazine. 68 (March 1798): 227.

Tytler, James. *An Answer to the Second Part of Paine's "Age of Reason."* London, 1797.

Scots Magazine. 59 (January 1797): 49–50.

Wakefield, Gilbert. *An Examination of "The Age of Reason," or an Investigation of True and Fabulous Theology of Thomas Paine.* Cambridge, 1794.

Analytical Review. 19 (June 1794): 165–70.

British Critic. 4 (December 1794): 684–85.

Critical Review. Ser. 2. 12 (September 1794): 111.

Evangelical Magazine. 3 (1795): 208–9.*

Gentleman's Magazine. 64 (July 1794): 642–44.

Monthly Review. N.s. 15 (October 1794): 339–42.

New Annual Register. 15 (1794): [177].

Protestant Dissenter's Magazine. 1 (1794): 461.*

———. *An Examination of "The Age of Reason," by Thomas Paine, with an Appendix of Remarks on a Letter from David Andrews. Second Edition, Corrected and Enlarged.* London, 1794.

Gentleman's Magazine. 64 (December 1794): 1117.

———. *A Reply to Paine's Second Part of "The Age of Reason."* London, 1795.

Analytical Review. 22 (December 1795): 598–603.

Critical Review. Ser. 2. 16 (March 1796): 319–25.

Gentleman's Magazine. 66 (October 1796): 852.

Monthly Review. N.s. 19 (January 1796): 161–65.

New Annual Register. 15 (1795): [198–99].

Protestant Dissenter's Magazine. 3 (1796): 37–38.*

Register of the Times. 7 (1795): 174–75.*

Walker's Hibernian Journal. Part 1 (1796): 118–22.*

Wallace, Elijah. *Universal Alarm or Age of Restoration . . . Being a Final Answer to Mr. T. Paine's "Age of Reason."* Dublin, 1798.

Waring, Jeremiah. *Three letters. Addressed to the Readers of Paine's "Age of Reason." By one of the People called Christians.* London, 1797.

Critical Review. Ser. 2. 21 (December 1797): 468.

New Annual Register. 18 (1797): [206–7].

Watson, Richard. *An Apology for the Bible. In a Series of Letters, Addressed to Thomas Paine, Author of a Book Entitled "The Age of Reason," Part the Second, Being an Investigation of True and Fabulous Theology.* London, 1796; Albany, 1796; Boston, 1796; New Brunswick, N.J., 1796.

Analytical Review. 24 (August 1796): 184–92.

British Critic. 7 (May 1796): 648–55.

English Review. 27 (April 1796): 465–70.

European Magazine. 29 (April 1796): 259–60.

Gentleman's Magazine. 66 (July 1796): 580–85.

Monthly Review. N.s. 20 (May 1796): 133–41.

Williams, John. *The Age of Infidelity: In Answer to Thomas Paine's "Age of Reason." By a Layman.* London, 1794.

Analytical Review. 19 (July 1794): 312–14.

British Critic. 4 (November 1794): 551.

Critical Review. Ser. 2. 13 (March 1795): 350–52.

English Review. 24 (July 1794): 123–24.

Evangelical Magazine. 3 (1795): 209–10.*

Gentleman's Magazine. 64 (November 1794): 1025–26.

Monthly Review. N.s. 15 (October 1794): 342.

New Annual Register. 15 (1794): [177–78].

Protestant Dissenter's Magazine. 1 (1794): 252, 379–80.*

———. *The Age of Infidelity: Part II. In Answer to the Second Part of "The Age of Reason"; With Some Additional Remarks on the Former. By a Layman.* London, 1796; Philadelphia, 1796.

Analytical Review. 23 (January 1796): 180–86.

British Critic. 8 (August 1796): 425–26.

Critical Review. Ser. 2. 16 (April 1796): 413–18.

Monthly Review. N.s. 20 (May 1796): 103–4.

Protestant Dissenter's Magazine. 3 (1796): 78–79.*

Wilmer, James Jones. *Consolation, Being a Replication to Thomas Paine, and Other Theologics.* Philadelphia, 1794.

Wilson, David. *Answer to Payne's "Age of Reason." With a Short View of the Obedience Which Christians Are Bound to Yield to the Powers That Be.* London, 1796.

British Critic. 9 (March 1797): 436–37.

Monthly Review. N.s. 22 (February 1797): 222.

Winchester, Elkanan. *A Defense of Revelation, in Ten Letters to Thomas Paine; Being an Answer to the First Part of "The Age of Reason."* London, 1796.

Analytical Review. 23 (March 1796): 261–63.

British Critic. 8 (July 1796): 184–85.

Critical Review. Ser. 2. 16 (April 1796): 405–12.

Freemason's Magazine. 6 (1796): 419.*

New Annual Register. 17 (1796): [177].

———. *Ten Letters Addressed to Mr. Paine, in Answer to His Pamphlet Entitled "The Age of Reason." Second Edition.* New York, 1795.

Notes

Introduction

1. It has been suggested, for instance, that the political emigrants from Britain and Ireland in the 1790s were carriers of a radical Painite message that supported the eventual dominance of the Jeffersonian republican image of a future America based on agriculture, commerce, and industry; see Michael Durey, "Thomas Paine's Apostles: Radical Émigrés and the Triumph of Jeffersonian Republicanism," *William and Mary Quarterly* 44 (1988): 661–88; Richard J. Twomey, *Jacobins and Jeffersonians: Anglo-American Radicalism in the United States, 1790–1820* (New York: Garland, 1989); and Isaac Kramnick, *Republicanism and Bourgeois Radicalism: Political Ideology in Late Eighteenth-Century England and America* (Ithaca: Cornell University Press, 1990).

2. Thomas W. Copeland, *Our Eminent Friend: Edmund Burke. Six Essays* (New Haven: Yale University Press, 1949), p. 148.

3. Of her listing of 340 publications concerning this controversy, Gayle Trusdel Pendleton concludes that 104 may be identified as reformist (Painean), while 213 may be considered as conservative (Burkean): "Towards a Bibliography of the *Reflections* and *Rights of Man* Controversy," *Bulletin of Research in the Humanities* 85 (1982): 65–103.

4. In fact, skepticism has been expressed concerning the influence of religious thought on Paine, as is evident in A. Owen Aldridge's otherwise quite useful *Thomas Paine's American Ideology* (Newark: University of Delaware Press, 1984).

5. Samuel Johnson, *The Rambler*, ed. W. J. Bate and Albrecht B. Strauss, in *The Works of Samuel Johnson* (New Haven: Yale University Press, 1969), 5:76. On the crisis of authority in revolutionary America, see Emory Elliott, *Revolutionary Writers: Literature and Authority in the New Republic, 1725–1810* (New York: Oxford University Press, 1982).

6. F. O'Gorman, *The Whig Party and the French Revolution* (New York: St. Martin's Press, 1967); Michael L. Kennedy, *The Jacobin Clubs in the French Revolution: The First Years* (Princeton: Princeton University Press, 1982), pp. 260–80; and J. G. A. Pocock, "Radical Criticism of the Whig Order in the Age between Revolutions," *The Origins of Anglo-American Radicalism*, ed. Margaret Jacob and James Jacob (London: Allen & Unwin, 1984), p. 49. Pocock notes, incidentally, that Paine is a difficult figure to place in this period (p. 48).

7. Sylvia Neely, *Lafayette and the Liberal Ideal, 1814–1824: Politics and Conspiracy in an Age of Reaction* (Carbondale and Edwardsville: Southern Illinois University Press, 1991), pp. 7–8.

8. W. T. Sherwin, *Memoir of the Life of Thomas Paine* (London: Richard Carlile, 1819), p. 94.

9. Richard Sennett, *The Fall of Public Man* (New York: Vintage, 1978), pp. 73–87, 107–22.

10. Alfred Owen Aldridge, *Man of Reason: The Life of Thomas Paine* (Philadelphia: J. B. Lippincott, 1959), p. 13. In *Thomas Paine: His Life, Work, and Times* (London: George Allen & Unwin, 1973), p. 24, however, Audrey Williamson suggests that the attraction between Paine and his father was based on the oppositeness of their personalities, a surmise we share. In human relations, opposites may attract, but they also conflict.

11. In *Identity: Youth and Crisis* (New York: W. W. Norton, 1968), Erik H. Erikson usefully differentiates between youthful *identification* with representatives within a hierarchy of roles and adolescent *identity formation* derived through selective (often totalistic) repudiation and often subtle assimilation of these roles. Although we by no means agree with all of Erikson's theories on identity, our study shares his understanding of identity as something continually in process of revision, unable to escape authoritative models, desirous of communal endorsement, and often engaged in paradoxical behavior.

12. C. John Sommerville, *The Discovery of Childhood in Puritan England* (Athens: University of Georgia Press, 1992), pp. 166–68. Whatever the personal implications of Paine's tax proposal, the plan also doubtless reflects French and English Jacobin concern with traditional familial patterns as obstacles to reform: see S. Maccoby, *English Radicalism, 1786–1832: From Paine to Cobbett* (London: Allen & Unwin), 1955.

13. Winthrop D. Jordan has suggested that *Common Sense* records a subliminal appeal to the psychological desire to kill the father that ironically ended with Paine becoming a father of his country; see "Familial Politics: Thomas Paine and the Killing of the King, 1776," *Journal of American History* 60 (1973): 294–308. Relatedly, in *Second Stories: The Politics of Language, Form, and Gender in Early American Fictions* (Chapel Hill: University of North Carolina Press, 1989), pp. 27–57, Cynthia S. Jordan observes that in his youthful acts of forgery and counterfeiting to improve on patriarchal political authority, Franklin inadvertently gives a glimpse of an underlying dissent from the suspect, merely fabricated authority he seems to valorize.

14. See Gary Kates, "From Liberalism to Radicalism: Tom Paine's *Rights of Man*," *Journal of the History of Ideas* 50 (1989): 569–87.

15. In this sense, our discussion supports, from another perspective, Evelyn J. Hinz's reading of the logical fallacies contained within Paine's demagogic appeal to reason, in "The 'Reasonable' Style of Tom Paine," *Queen's Quarterly* 79 (1972): 231–42. Hinz provides an overview of Paine's career in "Thomas Paine," in *American Literature, 1764–1789: The Revolutionary Years,* ed. Everett Emerson (Madison: University of Wisconsin Press, 1977), pp. 39–57. Pertinent, too, is Andrew Delbanco's argument that the Puritans in New England required a sense of oppositional force in maintaining their tenuous identity comprised of numerous tensions: *The Puritan Ordeal* (Cambridge: Harvard University Press, 1989).

16. Richard Sennett, *Authority* (New York: Knopf, 1980), pp. 20, 154.

17. Sennett, *Authority,* p. 27; cf. p. 192. On authority as an act of communication with fluid and relational terms, see the introductory remarks to *Authority,* ed. Carl Friedrich (Cambridge: Harvard University Press, 1958). On authority as a disguised reenactment by those who overcome their rulers, see Michel Foucault, "Nietzsche, Genealogy, History," in *Language, Counter-Memory, Practice,* ed. Donald F. Bouchard (Ithaca: Cornell University Press, 1977), p. 151.

18. On Paine's vision of humanity's ideal future, see Jack Fruchtman, Jr., "The Revolutionary Millennialism of Thomas Paine," *Studies in Eighteenth-Century Culture* 13

(1984): 65–77. See also "The Negative Structures of American Literature," *American Literature* 57 (1985): 1–22, in which Terence Martin detects in Paine's language a negative logic (characteristic of apophatic theology) that is destined to strip away the old to yield something like a blank slate permitting a sense of renewal in the reader.

19. On the contestatory relation between projection and criticism, identification and distance, and idealization and demystification as enabling features during the eighteenth century, see Fredric V. Bogel, *Literature and Substantiality in Later Eighteenth-Century England* (Princeton: Princeton University Press, 1984); and Bogel, *The Dream of My Brother: An Essay on Johnson's Authority* (Victoria, B.C.: University of Victoria English Literary Studies, 1990). On how the selection of a seal by deputies of the French National Convention recaptured and rehabilitated the representation of sovereign dominion and supremacy, the kingly power of old, see Lynn Hunt, "Hercules and the Radical Image in the French Revolution," *Representations* 2 (1983): 95–117.

20. Our view here suggests a sort of loneliness related, we believe, to Martin Roth's observation that the ideal of a self-determined America contains, as well, a melodrama of human isolation that presents humanity as lost in space and the present moment as exceeding the solace of an ideal American brotherhood: "Tom Paine and American Loneliness," *Early American Literatue* 22 (1988): 175–82.

21. Pertinently, in *Paine* (New York: Harper & Row, 1974), David F. Hawke argues that *The Age of Reason* is not restricted to the traditions of Anglo-American and French Deism.

22. See, typically, Karl Jaspers and Rudolf Bultmann, *Myth and Christianity: An Inquiry into the Possibility of Religion without Myth* (New York: Noonday Press, 1958); and *Kerygma and Myth: A Theological Debate,* ed. Hans Werner Bartsch (New York: Harper & Row, 1961).

23. See, representatively, Martin Dibelius and Hans Conzelmann, *The Pastoral Epistles* (Philadelphia: Westminster Press, 1972); and Helmut Koester, *History and Literature of Early Christianity* (Berlin: De Gruyth, 1982).

24. See, for example, Elaine Pagels, "The Politics of Paradise: Augustine's Exegesis of Genesis 1–3 Versus that of John Chrysostom," *Harvard Theological Review* 78 (1985): 67–95. See also, Gerd Tellenbach, *Church, State and Christian Society at the Time of the Investiture Contest,* trans. R. F. Bennett (New York: Harper & Row, 1970).

25. See, for example, Elaine Pagels, *Adam, Eve, and the Serpent* (New York: Random House, 1988).

Chapter 1. Young Paine and Biblical Authority

1. Dr. Alexander Hamilton, *The History of the Ancient and Honorable Tuesday Club,* ed. Robert Micklus (Chapel Hill: University of North Carolina Press, 1990), 1:144.

2. Pertinent studies of Franklin include, among recent entries, Mitchell Robert Breiwieser, *Cotton Mather and Benjamin Franklin: The Price of Representative Personality* (Cambridge: Cambridge University Press, 1984); Mark R. Patterson, *Authority, Autonomy and Representation in American Literature, 1776–1865* (Princeton: Princeton University Press, 1988), pp. 3–33; Ormond Seavey, *Becoming Ben Franklin: The "Autobiography" and the Life* (University Park: Pennsylvania State University Press, 1988); and Michael Warner, *The Letters of the Republic: Publication and the Public Sphere in Eighteenth-Century America* (Cambridge: Harvard University Press, 1990). On Jefferson, see James M. Cox, *Recovering Literature's Lost Ground: Essays in American Autobiography* (Baton

Rouge: Louisiana State University Press, 1989), pp. 33–54. See also William J. Scheick, "Benjamin Franklin and Lord Bute: Legendary Eighteenth-Cenury Representations," *Library Chronicle* 20, no. 3 (1990): 64–73. The period has also been called the Age of Contradiction: see Leon Howard, "The Late Eighteenth Century: An Age of Contradictions," in *Transitions in American Literary History,* ed. Harry Hayden Clark (Durham: University of North Carolina Press, 1953), pp. 51–89.

3. Francis Oldys, *The Life of Thomas Pain, the Author of the Seditious Writings Entitled the Rights of Man* (London: J. Stockdale, 1793), p. 7. Oldys was a pseudonym for George Chalmers (1742–1825), and his book (extremely hostile to Paine) went through ten editions and an abridgment by 1798. The tradition that Paine sought from Noble an introduction to the bishop of London with a view to ordination is given some weight by Ernest A. Payne's "Tom Paine: Preacher," *Times Literary Supplement,* no. 2365 (31 May 1947): 267. Paine's major biographer, Moncure Daniel Conway, suggested that "it is droll to think that the Church of England should ever [have] had an offer of Thomas Paine's services": *The Life of Thomas Paine* (New York: G. P. Putnam's Sons, 1908), 1:20.

4. Several studies explore various features of Quaker influence on Paine, including Robert P. Falk's "Thomas Paine: Deist or Quaker?" *Pennsylvania Magazine of History and Biography* 62 (1938): 52–63.

5. As quoted by Désirée Hirst, *Hidden Riches: Traditional Symbolism from the Renaissance to Blake* (London: Eyre & Spottiswood, 1964), p. 11.

6. That revolutionary and post-revolutionary rhetoric sometimes successfully integrated religious and political discouse is the subject of, among others, Donald Weber, *Rhetoric and History in Revolutionary New England* (New York: Oxford University Press, 1988).

7. It must be admitted that in a letter later appended to the third edition of *Common Sense* Paine berates the Quakers for "unwisely . . . mingling religion with politics" (2:60). This is, indeed, a contradictory moment, out of phase with his own procedure in the pamphlet. What Paine apparently means here is that the Quakers have mingled a particular, unwise component of their religious belief with politics.

8. On the possible influence of classical rhetorical theory on Paine's use of a selfless persona, see Jerome D. Wilson and William E. Ricketson, *Thomas Paine: Updated Edition* (Boston: Twayne, 1989), pp. 26–27.

Chapter 2. The Burke-Paine Controversy as Prelude

1. Paine took favorable notice of Price's *Observations* in the sixth *Crisis* paper (1:133).

2. Richard Price, *A Discourse on the Love of Our Country* (London: George Stafford, 1789), p. 40.

3. *Reflections on the Revolution in France,* in *The Writings and Speeches of the Right Honourable Edmund Burke* (Boston: Little, Brown, 1901), 3:301.

4. *The Correspondence of Edmund Burke,* ed. Alfred Cobban and Robert A. Smith (Cambridge: Cambridge University Press, 1967), 6:55n, 81.

5. Ibid., 6:71.

6. Alfred O. Aldridge provides the details of this undertaking in *Man of Reason: The Life of Thomas Paine* (Philadelphia: Lippincott, 1959), pp. 108–16. See also W. H. G. Armytage, "Thomas Paine and the Walkers: An Early Episode in Anglo-American Co-operation," *Pennsylvania History* 18 (1951): 22–24; and Paine, *Writings,* 2:1295–97.

7. Thomas Copeland, *Our Eminent Friend: Edmund Burke. Six Essays* (New Haven: Yale University Press, 1949), p. 156.

8. As Philip S. Foner indicates, *Writings,* 1:244n.

9. J. G. A. Pocock, "Radical Criticisms of the Whig Order in the Age between Revolutions," in *The Origins of Anglo-American Radicalism,* ed. Margaret Jacob and James Jacob (London: Allen & Unwin, 1984), pp. 49–51. That the marquis of Rockingham was similarly double-voiced is suggested in "British Ministers and American Resistance to the Stamp Act, October-December 1765," *William and Mary Quarterly* 49 (1992): 89–107, in which John L. Bullion revises Paul Langford's *First Rockingham Administration, 1765–1766* (Oxford: Oxford University Press, 1973).

10. Mrs. Aubrey Le Blond, *Charlotte Sophie, Countess Bemtinck* (London: Hutchinson, 1912), 1:163.

11. Burke, *Correspondence,* 6:141.

12. Paine's letter to Thomas Walker, printed in Armytage, "Paine and the Walkers," pp. 24–26.

13. Burke, *Correspondence,* 6:141.

14. See Aldridge, *Man of Reason,* p. 132.

15. Burke, *Correspondence,* 6:303–4.

16. The publishing history of Burke's *Reflections* is fully described by William B. Todd, *A Bibliography of Edmund Burke* (London: Rupert Hart-Davis, 1964), pp. 142–66. For the controversy provoked by Burke's book, see Carl B. Cone, "Pamphlet Replies to Burke's *Reflections,* " *Southwest Social Science Quarterly* 26 (1945–46): 23–34; James T. Boulton, *The Language and Politics in the Age of Wilkes and Burke* (London: Routledge & Kegan Paul, 1963), pp. 265–71; and R. R. Fennessy, *Burke, Paine, and the Rights of Man: A Difference of Political Opinion* (The Hague: Martinus Nijhoff, 1963), pp. 266–68. Boulton includes a chronological survey of eighty-nine replies to Burke's *Reflections* from 1790 to 1793 (pp. 265–71), and Fennessy provides an extensive paraphrase of Burke's argument (pp. 108–50). That of the 1,086 pamphlets published in England between July 1789 and the end of December 1793 at least 225 involved the controversy over *Reflections* and 325 involved Price, Burke, and Paine, is reported by Gayle T. Pendleton, "The English Pamphlet Literature of the Age of the French Revolution *Anatomized,* " *Eighteenth-Century Life* 5 (1978): 29–37.

17. Burke, *Second Letter on a Regicide Peace* (1796), in *Writings,* 5:345.

18. Burke, *Correspondence,* 6:173. As editors Cobban and Smith note, "Many of the revolutionaries professed a kind of sentimental Rousseauistic deism, but very few admitted to atheism" (6:173n).

19. Ibid., 6:71.

20. Burke, *Writings,* 3:244. John Quincy Adams published eleven letters in the Boston newspaper the *Columbian Sentinel* in June and July 1791. These letters replied to the first American edition of *The Rights of Man* and were reprinted in London in 1793 as *An Answer to Paine's Rights of Man.* Burke read them and found them quite to his taste (*Correspondence,* 7:504). For a contemporary review, see the *Analytical Review* 16 (May 1793): 203–7.

21. Burke, *Reflections,* in *Writings,* 3:244, 335. For a discussion of Burke and the revolutionaries, see passim Jeffrey Hart's "Burke and Radical Freedom," *Review of Politics,* 29 April 1967, 221–38; Burleigh Taylor Wilkins's *The Problem of Burke's Political Philosophy* (Oxford: Clarendon Press, 1967); Peter J. Stanlis's *Edmund Burke and the Natural Law* (Ann Arbor: University of Michigan Press, 1958); and Gerald W.

Chapman's *Edmund Burke: The Practical Imagination* (Cambridge: Harvard University Press, 1967).

22. Burke, *Writings*, 3:322.

23. Ibid., 3:331, 333. In *The Age of the Democratic Revolution* (Princeton: Princeton University Press, 1964), R. R. Palmer labels Burke's stature as a critic of the Revolution as "entirely a later construction" and his outbursts as dismaying to both his allies and opponents in Parliament (1:308, 309).

24. Burke, *Writings*, 3:369.

25. Significant inquiries into Burke's use of language include Chris Reid, "Language and Practice in Burke's Political Writing," in *Culture and Politics: From Puritanism to the Enlightenment,* ed. Perez Zagorin (Berkeley: University of California Press, 1980), pp. 244–46; and Steven Blakemore, *Burke and the Fall of Language: The French Revolution as Linguistic Event* (Hanover, N.H.: University Press of New England, 1988). See also John Turner, "Burke, Paine, and the Language of Assignats," *The Yearbook of English Studies* 19 (1989): 36–70.

26. Burke, *Writings*, 3:345.

27. E. P. Thompson, *The Making of the English Working Class* (New York: Pantheon, 1964), p. 99.

28. *The Genuine Trial of Thomas Paine, Author of the "Rights of Man," &c for a Libel; with the Eloquent Speeches of the Attorney General and Mr. Erskine on the Occasion,* taken in shorthand by E. Hodgson (London, 1792), pp. 4, 5.

29. At one point Erskine assailed the very nature of the proceedings: see *A Complete Collection of State Trials and Proceedings for High Treason and Other Crimes and Misdemeanors,* compiled by T. B. Howell and T. J. Howell (London: T. C. Hansard, 1816–28), 22:468.

30. *Analytical Review* 15 (January 1793): 189. On the subject of freedom of the press and libel, see Leonad W. Levy, *Emergence of a Free Press* (New York: Oxford University Press, 1985); and Jeffrey A. Smith, *Printers and Press Freedom: The Ideology of Early American Journalism* (New York: Oxford University Press, 1988).

31. Burke, *Writings*, 4:161.

32. A contemporary said of Paine: "This is no common man; this is the poor man's friend" (*Analytical Review* 12 [March 1792]: 304).

33. Burke, *Writings*, 3:385.

34. Fennessy offers a paraphrase of Paine's argument (pp. 160–80).

35. In "Republicanism versus Commercial Society: Paine, Burke, and the French Revolution Debate," *History of European Ideas* 11 (1989): 313–24, Gregory Claeys indicates that Paine's argument for economic equality, that republicanism was compatible with commerce, was a peripheral, weakly presented concern in his thinking and rejected by the main contributors to the debate.

36. Burke, *Writings*, 4:192.

37. Paine at one point speaks of Count Vergennes as "an aristocratic despot at home," and in the same paragraph claims "Mr. Burke's tribute of fear . . . runs parallel with Count Vergennes' refusal" (1:255–56), a typical instance of Paine's response to Burke's defense of royalty by associating him with monarchical despotism.

38. Carl B. Cone, *The English Jacobins: Reformers in 18th Century England* (New York: Charles Scribner's Sons, 1968) also notes that Burke's book determined the form of Paine's book (p. 97). In *Religion in England, 1688–1791* (Oxford: Clarendon, 1986), Gordon Rupp relatedly observes, "In 1791 two ultimate attitudes to human society were in

confrontation between Edmund Burke and Thomas Paine" (p. 554).

39. That Burke saw the French Revolution as a theatrical event and relied on the conventions of eighteenth-century drama in his discussion of it is discussed by Christopher Reid, Frans De Bruyn, and Thomas Eric Furniss in *Burke and the French Revolution: Bicentennial Essays,* ed. Steven Blakemore (Athens: University of Georgia Press, 1991).

Chapter 3. The Context of Paine's Biblical Learning

1. See, for example, Frank E. Manuel, *The Eighteenh Century Confronts the Gods* (Cambridge: Harvard University Press, 1959). On the tradition of scientific skepicism, which abetted biblical skepticism, see Richard H. Popkin, *The History of Scepticism from Erasmus to Descartes* (New York: Harper Torchbooks, 1968); and Margaret C. Jacob, *The Cultural Meaning of the Scientific Revolution* (Philadelphia: Temple University Press, 1988).

2. *The Life and Selected Letters of Thomas Jefferson,* ed. Adrienne Koch and William Peden (New York: Modern Library, 1944), pp. 431–33.

3. William Godwin, *The Adventures of Caleb Williams; or, Things As They Are* (London: Richard Bentley, 1835), p. xix.

4. Mary Wollstonecraft, *An Historical and Moral View of the Origin and Progress of the French Revolution; and the Effect It Has Produced in Europe* (London: J. Johnson, 1794), pp. 3–7.

5. *Analytical Review* 16 (June 1793): 186.

6. From 1777, when the English copyight was no longer observed, to 1800 there were only thirty-three editions of the entire Bible, but in the same period there were nearly eighty separate printings of the New Testament. Whereas the expression "The Bible" was slowly becoming identified with the New Testament alone, the Old Testament, on the other hand, was becoming identified with the book of Psalms. Although the Old Testament had no separate printings in the last three decades of the eighteenth century, the book of Psalms in various translations was frequently so printed. The most popular eighteenth-century edition of the Psalms in America was Isaac Watts's *Psalms of David. Imitated in the Language of the New Testament and Applied to the Christian State and Worship* (1719). His imitations, although entirely orthodox, consistently eliminate the darker sayings of David and stress in their place Christian consolation and comfort. The God of the Old Testament is refashioned in the image of the God of the New.

The Bible used for reference throughout this inquiry is *The Early Bible, Containing the Old and New Testamens: Newly Translated out of the Original Tongues; and with the Former Translations Diligently Compared and Revised. By His Majesty's Special Command Appointed to Be Read in CHURCHES* (London: Charles Bayne and William Strahan, 1766). Another clue to Paine's actual Bible appears in his citation of Deut. 25:4 concerning the "ox when he treadeth out the corn." Paine pointedly suggests that the verse "might not escape observation," except that the biblicists and "priests" have "noted" the verse "in the table of contents at the head of the chapter, though it is only a single verse of less than two lines" (1:524). The 1777 edition of the Bible we use marks that verse with apparent emphasis by citing it at the chapter's head: "The ox is not to be muzzled." And verse 25 also occupies "less than two lines," in fact, a line-and-a-half. None of the other verses in chapter 25 receive quite such attention at the head of the chapter. The other signature groupings are verses 1–3, 5–10, 11–12, 13–16, and 17–19.

7. On the intellectual connections between these cultures, see Peter Gay, *The Party of Humanity: Essays on the French Enlightenment* (New York: Knopf, 1964); and Gay, *The Enlightenment: An Interpretation* (New York: Knopf, 1969), 2:448–65.

8. It might be noted that in writing the first part of *The Age of Reason* Paine had well in mind arguments and issues that could be raised against Scripture to set forth what he called facts "too well established to be denied" (1:495). Where Paine did not have proper scriptural citations and quotations for part 1 nor had well in mind positions to take or answers to offer on biblical subjects he himself raised, he tended to rely on ancillary topics, which would, as it were, fill the gap and give authority to his strictures on the Bible and church. Contemporary astronomy was one such principle, as it was for Thomas Jefferson in his letter to Peter Carr. Paine knew astronomy as well as any intelligent, inquiring person of his day would know it. In the latter pages of part 1 he wrote an extended description of the physical universe that had replaced the narrow, provincial biblical universe (1:500–504). This description forms a declaration, a manifesto, in which the very extent and grandeur of the universe by simple contrast makes absurd (one of Paine's favorite words) the biblical Christian universe.

9. Benedict de Spinoza, *A Treatise Partly Theological, and Partly Political: The First English Edition* (London, 1689), p. 544.

10. *The Chief Works of Benedict de Spinoza*, trans. R. H. M. Elwes (New York: Dover, 1951), 1:135.

11. John Toland, *Christianity not Mysterious; or a Treatise Shewing that there is nothing in the Gospel Contrary to Reason* (London, 1696), p. 84.

12. Jeremiah Jones, *New and Full Method of Settling the Canonical Authority of the New Testament* (Oxford: Clarendon Press, 1798), 1:47.

13. Anthony Collins, *A Discourse of the Grounds and Reasons of the Christian Religion* (London: James and John Knapton, 1724), pp. 35–36.

14. Conyers Middleton, *The Miscellaneous Works* (London: R. Manby and H. S. Cox, 1752), 1:187.

15. Conyers Middleton, *A Free Inquiry into the Miraculous Powers Which Are Supposed to have Subsisted in the Christian Church, from the Earliest Ages through Several Successive Centuries* (London: R. Manby and H. S. Cox, 1749), pp. 57, 66.

16. See Edward Gibbon, *Memoirs of My Life*, ed. G. A. Bonnard (New York: Funk & Wagnalls, 1966), pp. 58–59.

17. *The British Museum Catalogue of Printed Books*, 24:643. *Examen critique* may have appeared in a different form. At one place in *The Age of Reason* Paine states that his quotations were taken "from the second chapter" of Boulanger's work (1:587n). His version is almost word for word identical to the English translation of 1823, a fact that shows Paine's effectiveness in translating French.

18. See Manuel, *The Eighteenth Century*; Alan Charles Kors, *D'Holbach's Coterie: An Enlightenment in Paris* (Princeton: Princeton University Press, 1976).

19. *Critical Examination of the Life of St. Paul, Translated from the French of Boulanger* (London: R. Carlile, 1823), pp. 7–8.

20. Ibid., pp. 64, 5, 41.

21. Leslie Chard II, "Joseph Johnson: Father of the Book Trade," *Bulletin of the New York Public Library* 79 (1975): 51–82. On Johnson, see also Claire Tomalin, *The Life and Death of Mary Wollstonecraft* (New York: Harcourt Brace Jovanovich, 1974), pp. 66–82. For a concise history of the *Analytical Review*, see *British Literary Magazines: The Augustan Age and the Age of Johnson, 1698–1788*, ed. Alvin Sullivan (Westport, Conn.:

Greenwood Press, 1983), pp. 11–14. For a bibliography and brief discussion of religious magazines at the time, see Samuel J. Rogal, "Religious Periodicals in England during the Restoration and Eighteenth Century," *Journal of the Rutgers University Library* 35 (1971): 27–33.

22. Alexander Gilchrist, *Life of William Blake* (London: Everyman's Library, 1942), p. 82. See also, Moncure Daniel Conway, *The Life of Thomas Paine* (New York: G. P. Putnam's Sons, 1908), 1:351. On Blake's life and thought at this time of the early stages of the French Revolution, see Burton R. Friedman, *Fabricating History: English Writers on the French Revolution* (Princeton: Princeton University Press, 1988): pp. 38–66.

23. *William Blake's Writings,* ed. G. E. Bentley, Jr. (Oxford: Clarendon Press, 1978), pp. 1404, 1410, 1412, 1424. In "William Blake, Thomas Paine, and the Biblical Revolution," *Studies in Romanticism* 30 (1991): 189–212, Robert N. Essick measures the influence of the biblical hermeneutics of Johnson's circle by comparing mutual thematic matter and verbal echoes in *The Marriage of Heaven and Hell* and writings by Paine.

24. Alexander Geddes, *Prospectus of a New Translation of the Holy Bible* (Glasgow and London: privately printed, 1786), p. 19.

25. Alexander Geddes, *Dr. Geddes's Address to the Public on the Publication of the First Volume of His New Translation of the Bible* (London: privately printed, 1793), p. 6.

26. Geddes, *Prospectus,* p. xx.

27. The full title page of Geddes's translation reads *The Holy Bible, or the Books Accounted Sacred by the Jews and Chistians, Otherwise Called the Books of the Old and New Covenants, Faithfully Translated from the Original; with Various Readings, Explanatory Notes, and Critical Remarks.* By the Reverend Alexander Geddes. Printed for the Author. London, 1792. The British Museum Catalogue notes, "No more published"; but there was a second volume published in 1797. For a very hostile review of this work, see *The Anti-Jacobin Review* 3 (May 1799): 1–8.

28. *Dr. Geddes's General Answer to the Queries, Councils, and Criticisms That Have Been Communicated to Him Since the Publication of His Proposals for Printing a New Translation of the Bible* (London: J. Davis, 1790), p. 5. It is to be noted that this pamphlet of thirty pages was printed by Johnson. Geddes publicly protested the suppression of his translation of the Bible in *Letter from the Rev. A. G., LL.D. to the Right Rev. John Douglass, Bishop of Centuriae, and Vicar Apostolic in the London District* (London: R. Faulder, 1794). See W. Neil, "The Criticism and Theological Use of the Bible, 1700–1950," in *Cambridge History of the Bible,* ed. S. L. Greenslade (Cambridge: Cambridge University Press, 1962), 3:272.

29. See, for instance, Jerome McGann, "The Idea of an Indeterminate Text: Blake's Bible of Hell and Dr. Alexander Geddes," *Studies in Romanticism* 25 (1986): 303–24.

30. A contemporary summary of the Geddes controversy appears in *Gentleman's Magazine* 65 (January 1795): 9–10.

31. *Dr. Geddes's Address,* p. 2. See also Hans Frei, *The Eclipse of Biblical Narrative* (New Haven: Yale University Press, 1974).

32. Geddes, preface to *The Holy Bible*, p. xi.

Chapter 4. Paine Reads the Bible

1. A detailed inquiry into biblical commentary in the eighteenth century is provided by Thomas P. Preston, "Biblical Criticism Literature, and the Eighteenth-Century Reader," in

Books and Their Readers in Eighteenth-Century England, ed. Isabel Rivers (New York:St. Martin's Press, 1982), pp. 97–126. See also Robert M. Grant and David Tracy, *A Short History of the Interpretation of the Bible* (Philadelphia: Fortress Press, 1963); and Robert Morgan and John Barton, *Biblical Interpretation* (Oxford: Oxford University Press, 1988).

2. Whether Paine knew the "Bible Chronology" he used was the creation of Bishop Ussher remains uncertain. In the years of the publication of *The Age of Reason* and the attendant controversy, three large and imposing chronologies appeared: Robert Walker's *Analysis of Researches into the Origin and Progress of Historical Time* (London, 1796), Philip Howard's *The Scripture History of the Earth and Mankind* (London, 1797), and Thomas Falconer's *Chronological Tables* (London, 1796). They reviewed all the dates provided by scriptural and pagan history and confirmed the chronological scheme of Ussher. The reviews of these works signify the wide acceptance of this system of dating, one review even concluding that "divine truth shall gain a full ascendancy by its native energy" (*Critical Review* 23 [1797]: 180). There is no hint of the existence of any forces aimed at undercuting and destroying such systems of chronology. See, for example, *Critical Review* 23 (1798): 169–80; and *Gentleman's Magazine* 66 (1796): 762–65.

3. Traditional arguments for the Mosaic authorship of the Pentateuch rested on the principle that Ezra could not have been the composer because he himself ascribed the books of the law to Moses (Ezra 3:2), that every subsequent book of the Old Testament implies and relies on the existence of the Pentateuch (Josh. 1:7, 8; 8:31; 23;6; 1 Kings 2:3; 2Kings 14:6; 2 Chron. 17:9; 24:6); that Hebrew ceased to be a living language among the Israelites before or about the time of the Babylonian Captivity; and that the law of Moses was deposited in the Temple and read to the people every seventh year from the time of its bestowal to the setting down of the record (Deut. 31:10, 24).

4. Curiously, Paine makes no mention of the two disinct accounts of the Creation in the first two chapers of Genesis, a problem well known in intellectual circles of Paine's time and supportive of his case against the literal accuracy of the Pentateuch. However, in defending himself in his "Letter to Mr. Erskine" (1797), addressed to the barrister who prosecuted the publisher of *The Age of Reason,* Paine clearly distinguishes between the two accounts in Genesis. "Here are," he concludes, "two different stories contradicting each other" (2:731), a point he repeated in his "Reply to the Bishop of Llandaff" (2:764–65).

5. Even with a copy of the Bible at hand, Paine nearly himself invents a passage of Scripture when he describes David's taking of Jerusalem (1 Chron. 5:4ff.; 14:4ff.) as evidencing a bloodthirstiness not supported by the biblical account: "It is not said . . . that they *utterly destroyed men, women, and children; that they left not a soul to breathe,* as is said of their other conquests" (1:535). Paine may have made up this seeming quotation out of Josh. 11:11–14 and 1 Sam. 27:9, where the vengefulness is nearly as strong as expressed in Paine's invented verse.

6. The argument for prophecy had been set forth with great vigor in Samuel Clarke's Boyle lectures of 1705; as he wrote in the ninth edition of *A Discourse Concerning the Being and Attributes of God, the Obligations of Natural Religion, and the Truth and Certainty of the Christian Revelation* (London: James and John Knapton, 1738), p. 371, Christian prophecy "*is positively and directly proved, to be actually and immediately sent to us from God, by the many infallible Signs and Miracles which the Author of it worked publickly as the evidence of his Divine Commission.*" For the savants and biblical scholars of the eighteenth century, the controversy concerning prophecy began in 1724, when the mathematician William Whiston published a tract that provided Anthony Collins with an

opportunity to attack the argument from prophecy in his *Discouse of the Grounds and Reasons of the Christian Religion* (1724). The major treatment of prophecy, especially in respect to Paine's handling of the subject, was Nathaniel Lardner's *Credibility of the Gospel History* (1730), which disclosed that the Old Testament prophecies were fulfilled in the New Testament and were, in turn, confirmed by passages of ancient authors who were contemporary with Jesus and the apostles or who lived not long afterward. Lardner offered testimony from the earliest church fathers down through the saints and martyrs to the time of Constantine the Great and the Councils, including Josephus and opponents, to the year 1325, all showing that the prophetic scheme of Scripture was infallible and confirmed by every testimony.

7. This tragic outcome was not relevant to Isaiah 7 nor to the prophecy of the virgin and the child. By the verses concerning the defeat of Ahaz, Paine saw in his Bible a small-print, italicized reference to 2 Chron. 28, to which he apparently turned and there found what had happened to Ahaz. Matthew, who is surely the first to do so, takes the word *virgin* in the prophecy to mean specifically the Virgin Mary and thus introduced a miraculous element into what was meant by the prophet to be simply a way of measuring time between the virgin's conceiving and of the land's coming into production and fruition. Paine, however, reverses the process and speaks of the "lying prophet" who devised such a "barefaced perversion of this story, that the book of Matthew, and the impudence and the . . . sordid interests of priests in later times, have founded a theory which they call the Gospel . . . 700 years after this foolish story was told" (1:555).

8. Paine apparently discovered this discrepancy by following the marginal reference in his Bible that linked Jer. 37:11–13 with Jer. 21:1–8 and 38:1–17. So the prophet, in Paine's view, stood condemned of falsehood by his own words, or in the words given to him by others long afterward.

9. He also rules against the book of Jonah, which he reads as a simple tale of how a Jew was treated by Gentiles and as a critique of prophecy itself: "As a moral, it preaches against the malevolent spirit of prediction; for as certainly as a man predicts ill, he becomes inclined to wish it" (1:569). And of the minor prophets, Paine claims they were only "itinerant preachers who mixed poetry, anecdote, and devotion together" (1:477).

10. The "Harmonists" were a number of leading expositors and defenders of Scripture who responded to the attacks of the Deists. Their chief works included Philip Doddridge's six-volume *The Family Expositer* (1739–56), Thomas Townson's *Discourse on the Evangelical History* (1793), and James Mcknight's *Harmony of the Gospels* (1778). Joseph Priestley criticized the last volume in *A Harmony of the Evangelists* (1780), and for a time he engaged in a series of *Letters* with Newcome, archbishop of Armagh.

11. For an authoritative account, in Paine's time, of the fixing of the canon of the New Testament and the recognition of Christianity as the official religion of the Roman Empire, see William Paley, *A View of the Evidences of Christianity* (London: R. Faulder, 1794), 2:199–203.

Chapter 5. Paine Is Answered

1. That the significance of Paine's endeavor was minor in comparison to the conservative religious force—a conclusion with which we disagree—is advanced by Martin Fitzpatrick, "Heretical Religion and Radical Political Ideas in Late Eighteenth-Century

England," in *The Transformation of Political Culture: England and Germany in the Late Eighteenth Century,* ed. Eckhart Hellmuth (London: Oxford University Press and German Historical Institute, 1990), pp. 339–72.

2. "The Deists," Gordon Rupp has observed in *Religion in England, 1688–1791* (Oxford: Clarendon Press, 1986), p. 277, were "a self-conscious elite": "upper class aristocrats like Shaftesbury and Bolingbroke, and the landed gentleman Anthony Collins, dons like Woolston and Tindal, and the medical man, Thomas Morgan." While there was something rightly called *deism* in and behind Paine's thinking, it is a deism of a general kind. Paine held certain strong, simple beliefs, which shared a number of features with intellectual Deism during his time. However, if *The Age of Reason* is read primarily as a deistical statement, then it must also be read as a belated one at the end of the eighteenth century, when Deism was fading and on the verge of disappearing. Paine did sign himself as "A True Deist" in one of his public papers in 1804 (2:806), and as "A Member of the Deistical Church" in another paper in which he defined "Deism [as] the only profession of religion that admits of worshiping and reverencing God in purity, and the only one on which he thoughtful mind can repose with undistubed tranquility" (2:811). On various eighteenth-century distinctions between *deism* and *atheism,* see Frank E. Manuel, *The Eighteenth Century Confronts the Gods* (Cambridge: Harvard University Press, 1959); Alan Charles Kors, *D'Holbach's Coterie: An Enlightenment in Paris* (Princeton: Princeton University Press, 1976); and Kors, *Atheism in France, 1650–1729* (Princeton: Princeton University Press, 1990).

3. *Gentleman's Magazine* 66 (October 1796): 397; 65 (July 1795): 598. For a review of the vicissitudes of Paine's reputation in later times, see Jerome D. Wilson, "Thomas Paine in America: An Annotated Bibliography, 1900–1973," *Bulletin of Bibliography* 31 (1974): 133–56, 180.

4. Richard Watson, *The Apology for the Bible* (New York: T. & J. Swords, 1796), p. 56.

5. Watson, *Apology,* p. iv.

6. Gilbert Wakefield, *An Examination of the Age of Reason* (Worcester, Mass.: Isaiah Thomas, 1794), pp. 1, 26.

7. Joseph Priestley, *Letters to a Philosophical Unbeliever* (Cambridge, 1823), pp. 138, 167; this edition contains Priestley's *An Answer to M. Paine's Age of Reason.* On Priestley's rejoinder to *The Age of Reason,* see Michael Payne, "Priestley, Paine, Blake, and the Tradition of English Dissent," *Pennsylvania English* 10 (1983): 5–13.

8. Priestley, *Letters,* p. 167.

9. Levi, like Elias Boudinot, also worried that the French Revolution and the Painite message derived from it might mean the close of providential history: see Richard H. Popkin, "*The Age of Reason* versus *The Age of Revelation*: Two Critics of Tom Paine," in *Deism, Masonry, and The Enlightenment,* ed. J. A. Leo Lemay (Newark: University of Delaware Press, 1987), pp. 158–70.

10. David Levi, *Defence of the Old Testament, in a Series of Letters Addressed to Thomas Paine* (New York: William A. Davis, 1797), pp. 162–63, 56, 150.

11. James T. Boulton, *The Language of Politics in the Age of Wilkes and Burke* (London: Routledge & Kegan Paul, 1963), pp. 265–71.

12. Timothy Dwight, *The Nature and Danger of Infidel Philosophy* (New Haven: George Bunce, 1798), p. 64.

13. Richard Whately, *Essays on Some of the Dangers to Christian Faith* (London, B. Fellows, 1839), p. 108.

14. *Critical Review,* ser. 2, 19 (1797): 464.

15. John Jamieson, *An Alarm to Britain; or, an Inquiry into the Causes of the Rapid Progress of Infidelity, in the Present Age* (Perth: R. Morrison, Jr., 1795), p. 46; as quoted in *Gentleman's Magazine* 68 (April 1798): 292.

16. *Hints; or A Short Account of the Principal Movers of the French Revolution* (London, 1794), as quoted in the *Analytical Review* 18 (Feb./May 1794): 220.

17. Thomas Taylor, *A Vindication of the Rights of Brutes* (Boston: B. Sweetser and W. Burdick, 1795), p. 10.

18. Whately, *Essays,* pp. 77–78, 81, 108.

19. Burke, *Writings,* 3:335. See Boulton, *The Language of Politics,* p. 259. On the radical tradition affecting the religion of the working class as expressed in *The Age of Reason,* see Edward Royle, *Radical Politics, 1790–1900: Religion and Unbelief* (London: Longman, 1971), pp. 3–22; and on the pertinent pervasiveness of an evangelical, popular democratic insurgency during these times, see Nathan O. Hatch, *The Democratization of American Christianity* (New Haven: Yale University Press, 1989).

20. In *The Making of the English Working Class* (New York: Pantheon, 1964), p. 127, E. P. Thompson has suggested, however, that there was a "sea-change in the attitudes of the inarticulate" and "in the structure of feeling of the poor," both of which disposed people during the 1790s "to harbour and tolerate the seditious."

21. *Analytical Review* 21 (March 1795): 304.

22. The anointing of kings with holy oil and the practice of the holy touch, for example, were important elements in the development of the idea of the sacred nature of kings and priests in England and France; see R. W. Carlyle and A. J. Carlyle, *A History of the Medieval Political Theory in the West* (Edinburgh: Blackwood & Sons, 1936), 4:185–91, 271–92, 429–61.

23. Robert Gray, *Sermons on the Principles upon which the Reformation of the Church of England was Established* (London: Rivingtons and Robson, 1796).

Conclusion: "I Can Write a Better Book Myself"

1. S. R. F. Price, *Rituals and Power: The Roman Imperial Cult in Asia Minor* (Cambridge: Cambridge University Press, 1984), p. 242.

2. Frederick B. Tolles, *Quakers and the Atlantic Culture* (New York: Macmillan, 1960), p. 107.

3. See Daniel B. Shea, Jr., *Spiritual Autobiography in Early America* (Princeton: Princeton University Press, 1968), pp. 3–84. We have relied on Shea throughout our application of the taxonomy of Quaker confession.

4. Relatedly, in *The Complex Image: Faith and Method in American Autobiography* (Philadelphia: University of Pennsylvania Press, 1989), pp. 83–115, Joseph Fichtelberg observes how Franklin reduces himself to a cipher, after the manner of earlier spiritual relations, so that he can mutate his voice in response to his sense of changing audiences. Mutation of voice is also featured in Mary Cappello's "Authority of Self-Definition in Thomas Shepard's *Autobiography* and *Journal,*" *Early American Literature* 24 (1989): 35–51.

5. Oddly, Paine ignores the scriptural passage in which Noah's son Ham sees his father naked and drunk, for which act Noah later curses Ham's son Canaan: "a servant of servants shall he be unto his brethren" (Gen. 9:25). This text was used by modern

Europeans to justify the translation of Africans into slaves in America. Before *The Age of Reason* Paine had attacked slavery in "African Slavery in America" (1775) and "Emancipation of Slaves" (1779), and presumably he was well aware of the use of Scripture as an authorization for what Melville would later characterize in "Misgivings" (1860) as "man's foulest crime" weakening "the world's fairest hope" (America as an ark in the deluge "from the waste of Time").

6. See Benedict Anderson, *Imagined Communities: Reflections on the Origin and Spread of Nationalism* (London: Verso Editions, 1983), p. 30. That eighteenth-century newspapers and periodicals could encourage their working-class audience to think of itself as participating in a political elite culture is noted by David Paul Nord, "A Republican Literature: Magazine Reading and Readers in Late-Eighteenth-Century New York," in *Reading in America: Literature and Social History,* ed. Cathy N. Davidson (Baltimore: Johns Hopkins University Press, 1989), pp. 114–39.

7. See John Owen King III, *The Iron of Melancholy: Structures of Spiritual Conversion in America from the Puritan Conscience to Victorian Neurosis* (Middletown, Conn.: Wesleyan University Press, 1983).

8. Paul Ricoeur, *The Conflict of Interpretations: Essays in Hermeneutics* (Evanston, Ill.: Northwestern University Press, 1974), pp. 269–96.

9. See Patricia Caldwell, *The Puritan Conversion Narrative: The Beginnings of American Expression* (Cambridge: Cambridge University Press, 1983), pp. 31, 121–22, 163–86.

10. See, for example, Emory Elliott, *Revolutionary Writers: Literature and Authority in the New Republic, 1725–1810* (New York: Oxford University Press, 1982); and Robert S. Levine, *Conspiracy and Romance: Studies in Brockden Brown, Cooper, Hawthorne, and Melville* (Cambridge: Cambridge University Press, 1989), pp. 1–15. Pertinent here, as well, is the John A. Kouwenhoven's argument concerning the national preoccupation with process in America: *Made in America: The Arts in Modern American Civilization* (New York: W. W. Norton, 1967).

11. In "Parasiting America: The Radical Function of Heterogeneity in Thomas Paine's Early Writings," *Eighteenth-Century Studies* 25 (1992): 331–51, Molly Anne Rothenberg observes that Paine's figure of the parasite represents the processive negotiation of personal and cultural contradictions.

Appendix 1. The Composition of *The Age of Reason*

1. A few years afterward, Paine described rather nostalgically the rooms he occupied in the rue Faubourg, St. Denis, in 1793 (2:1125). The most detailed account of Paine's time in France during the Revolution is provided by David Freeman Hawke, *Paine* (New York: Harper & Row, 1974), pp. 256–327. On the activities of Paine and his colleagues at this time, see John G. Alger, *Paris in 1789–1794* (London: G. Allen, 1902), pp. 325–28; and Nicholas Roe, *Wordsworth and Coleridge: The Radical Years* (Oxford: Clarendon Press, 1988), pp. 130–31.

2. Hawke, *Paine,* 360.

3. See Aldridge, *Man of Reason: The Life of Thomas Paine* (Philadelphia: J. B. Lippincott, 1959), p. 208; and Robert F. Durden, "Joel Barlow in the French Revolution," *William and Mary Quarterly* 8 (1951): 327–54.

4. Richard Gimbel, "The First Appearance of Thomas Paine's *The Age of Reason*," *Yale University Library Gazette* 31 (1956): 87.

5. Moncure Daniel Conway, *The Life of Thomas Paine* (New York: G. P. Putnam's Sons, 1908), 2:236.

6. Gimbel, "First Appearance," 87.

7. See Richard Gimbel, "The Resurgence of Thomas Paine," *Proceedings of the American Antiquarian Society* 69 (1960): 429–33.

8. See Emily Ellsworth Ford Steel, *Mason Locke Weems: His Works and Ways in Three Volumes: A Bibliography Left Unfinished by Paul Leicester Ford* (New York: privately printed, 1929), 1:295–96.

9. *The Works of Thomas Paine* (Philadelphia, 1797), 1, sig. A[4].

Works Cited

Aldridge, Alfred Owen. *Man of Reason: The Life of Thomas Paine.* Philadelphia: J. B. Lippincott, 1959.

——. *Thomas Paine's American Ideology.* Newark: University of Delaware Press, 1984.

Alger, John G. *Paris in 1789–1794.* London: G. Allen, 1902.

Anderson, Benedict. *Imagined Communities: Reflections on the Origin and Spread of Nationalism.* London: Verso Editions, 1983.

Armytage. W. H. G. "Thomas Paine and the Walkers: An Early Episode in Anglo-American Co-operation." *Pennsylvania History* 18 (1951): 22–24.

Bartsch, Hans Werner, ed. *Kerygma and Myth: A Theological Debate.* New York: Harper & Row, 1961.

Blake, William. *William Blake's Writings.* Edited by G. E. Bentley, Jr. Oxford: Clarendon Press, 1978.

Blakemore, Steven. *Burke and the Fall of Language: The French Revolution as Linguistic Event.* Hanover, N.H.: University Press of New England, 1988.

——, ed. *Burke and the French Revolution: Bicentennial Essays.* Athens: University of Georgia Press, 1991.

Bogel, Fredric V. *The Dream of My Brother: An Essay on Johnson's Authority.* Victoria, B.C.: University of Victoria English Literary Studies, 1990.

——. *Literature and Substantiality in Later Eighteenth-Century England.* Princeton: Princeton University Press, 1984.

Bouchard, Donald F., ed. *Language, Counter-Memory, Practice.* Ithaca: Cornell University Press, 1977.

Boulton, James T. *The Language of Politics in the Age of Wilkes and Burke.* London: Routledge & Kegan Paul, 1963.

Breitwieser, Mitchell Robert. *Cotton Mather and Benjamin Franklin: The Price of Representative Personality.* Cambridge: Cambridge University Press, 1984.

Bullion, John L. "British Ministers and American Resistance to the Stamp Act, October-December, 1765." *William and Mary Quarterly* 49 (1992): 89–107.

Burke, Edmund. *The Correspondence of Edmund Burke.* 10 vols. Edited by Alfred Cobban and Robert A. Smith. Cambridge: Cambridge University Press, 1958–78.

——. *The Writings and Speeches of the Right Honourable Edmund Burke.* 5 vols. Boston: Little, Brown, 1901.

Caldwell, Patricia. *The Puritan Conversion Narrative: The Beginnings of American Expression.* Cambridge: Cambridge University Press, 1983.

Cappello, Mary. "The Authority of Self-Definition in Thomas Shepard's *Autobiography* and *Journal.*" *Early American Literature* 24 (1989): 35–51.

Carlyle, R. W., and A. J. Carlyle. *A History of Medieval Poltical Theory in the West.* 6 vols. Edinburgh: Blackwood & Sons, 1936.

Chapman, Gerald W. *Edmund Burke: The Practical Imagination.* Cambridge: Harvard University Press, 1967.

Chard, Leslie II. "Joseph Johnson: Father of the Book Trade." *Bulletin of the New York Public Library* 79 (1975): 51–82.

Claeys, Gregory. "Republicanism versus Commercial Society: Paine, Burke and the French Revolution Debate." *History of European Ideas* 11 (1989): 313–24.

Clarke, Samuel. *A Discourse Concerning the Being and Attributes of God, the Obligations of Natural Religion, and the Truth and Certainty of the Christian Revelation.* London: James and John Knapton, 1738.

Collins, Anthony. *Discourse of the Grounds and Reasons of the Christian Religion.* London: James and John Knapton, 1724.

Cone, Carl B. *The English Jacobins: Reformers in 18th Century England.* New York: Charles Scribner's Sons, 1968.

————. "Pamphlet Replies to Burke's *Reflections.*" *Southwest Social Science Quarterly* 26 (1945–46): 23–34.

Conway, Moncure Daniel. *The Life of Thomas Paine.* 2 vols. New York: G. P. Putnam's Sons, 1908.

Copeland, Thomas W. *Our Eminent Friend: Edmund Burke: Six Essays.* New Haven: Yale University Press, 1949.

Cox, James M. *Recovering Literature's Lost Ground: Essays in American Autobiography.* Baton Rouge: Louisiana State University Press, 1989.

Davidson, Edward H., and William J. Scheick. "Authority in Paine's *Common Sense* and *Crisis Papers.*" *Studies in the Humanities* 18 (1991): 124–34.

Delbanco, Andrew. *The Puritan Ordeal.* Cambridge: Harvard University Press, 1989.

Dibelius, Martin, and Hans Conzelmann. *The Pastoral Epistles.* Philadelphia: Westminster Press, 1972.

Doddridge, Philip. *The Family Expositer.* 2 vols. Hartford: Lincoln and Gleason, 1807.

Durden, Robert F. "Joel Barlow in the French Revolution." *William and Mary Quarterly* 8 (1951): 327–54.

Durey, Michael. "Thomas Paine's Apostles: Radical Émigrés and the Triumph of Jeffersonian Republicanism." *William and Mary Quarterly* 44 (1987): 661–88.

Dwight, Timothy. *The Nature and Danger of Infidel Philosophy.* New Haven: George Bunce, 1798.

The Early Bible, Containing the Old and New Testaments: Newly Translated out of the Original Tongues; and with the Former Translations Diligently Compared and Revised. By His Majesty's Special Command Appointed to Be Read in CHURCHES. London: Charles Bayne and William Strahan, 1766.

Elliott, Emory. *Revolutionary Writers: Literature and Authority in the New Republic, 1725–1810.* New York: Oxford University Press, 1982.

Erikson, Erik H. *Identity: Youth and Crisis.* New York: W. W. Norton, 1968.

Essick, Robert N. "William Blake, Thomas Paine, and the Biblical Revolution." *Studies in Romanticism* 30 (1991): 189–212.

Falconer, Thomas. *Chronological Tables.* Oxford, 1796.

Falk, Robert P. "Thomas Paine: Deist or Quaker?" *Pennsylvania Magazine of History and Biography* 62 (1938): 52–63.

Fennessy, R. R. *Burke, Paine, and the Rights of Man: A Difference of Political Opinion.* The Hague: Martinus Nijhoff, 1963.

Fichtelberg, Joseph. *The Complex Image: Faith and Method in American Autobiography.* Philadelphia: University of Pennsylvania Press, 1989.

Fitzpatrick, Martin. "Heretical Religion and Radical Political Ideas in Late-Eighteenth-Century England." In *The Transformation of Political Culture: England and Germany in the Late Eighteenth Century,* edited by Eckhart Hellmuth, 339–72. London: Oxford University Press and German Historical Institute, 1990.

Frei, Hans. *The Eclipse of Biblical Narrative.* New Haven: Yale University Press, 1974.

Friedman, Burton R. *Fabricating History: English Writers on the French Revolution.* Princeton: Princeton University Press, 1988.

Friedrich, Carl, ed. *Authority.* Cambridge: Harvard University Press, 1958.

Fruchtman, Jack, Jr. "The Revolutionary Millennialism of Thomas Paine." *Studies in Eighteenth-Century Culture* 13 (1984): 65–77.

Gay, Peter. *The Enlightenment: An Interpretation.* New York: Knopf, 1969.

———. *The Party of Humanity: Essays on the French Enlightenment.* New York: Knopf, 1964.

Geddes, Alexander. *Dr. Geddes's Address to the Public on the Publication of the First Volume of His New Translation of the Bible.* London: privately printed, 1793.

———. *Dr. Geddes's General Answer to the Queries, Councils, and Criticisms That Have Been Communicated to Him Since the Publication of His Proposals for Printing a New Translation of the Bible.* London: J. Davis, 1790.

———. *Letter from the Rev. A. G., LL.D. to the Right Rev. John Douglass, Bishop of Centuriae, and Vicar Apostolic in the London District.* London: R. Faulder, 1794.

———. *Prospectus of a New Testament of the Holy Bible.* Glasgow and London: privately printed, 1786.

———, trans. *The Holy Bible, or the Books Accounted Sacred by the Jews and Christians, Otherwise Called the Books of the Old and New Covenants, Faithfully Translated from the Original; with Various Readings, Explanatory Notes, and Critical Remarks.* London: privately printed, 1792.

The Genuine Trial of Thomas Paine, Author of the "Rights of Man," &c for a Libel; with the Eloquent Speeches of the Attorney General and Mr. Erskine on the Occasion. London, 1792.

George, Mary Dorothy. *Catalogue of Political and Personal Satires.* Vol. 7: *1793– 1800.* London: British Museum, 1942.

Gibbon, Edward. *Memoirs of My Life.* Edited by G. A. Bonnard. New York: Funk & Wagnalls, 1966.

Gilchrist, Alexander. *Life of William Blake.* London: Everyman's Library, 1942.

Gimbel, Richard. "The First Appearance of Thomas Paine's *The Age of Reason.*" *Yale University Library Gazette* 31 (1956): 87–89.

———. "The Resurgence of Thomas Paine." *Proceedings of the American Antiquarian Society* 69 (1960): 429–33.

Godwin, William. *The Adventures of Caleb Williams; or, Things As They Are.* London: Richard Bentley, 1835.

Grant, Robert M., and David Tracy. *A Short History of the Interpretation of the Bible.* Philadelphia: Fortress Press, 1963.

Gray, Robert. *Sermons on the Principles upon which the Reformation of the Church of England was Established.* London: Rivingtons and Robson, 1796.

Greenslade, S. L., ed. *Cambridge History of the Bible.* 3 vols. Cambidge: Cambridge University Press, 1962–78.

Hamilton, Dr. Alexander. *The History of the Ancient and Honorable Tuesday Club.* 2 vols. Edited by Robert Micklus. Chapel Hill: University of North Carolina Press, 1990.

Hart, Jeffrey. "Burke and Radical Freedom." *Review of Politics* 29 (April 1967): 221–38.

Hatch, Nathan O. *The Democratization of American Christianity.* New Haven: Yale University Press, 1989.

Hawke, David Freeman. *Paine.* New York: Harper & Row, 1974.

Hinz, Evelyn J. "The 'Reasonable' Style of Tom Paine." *Queen's Quarterly* 79 (1972): 231–42.

———. "Thomas Paine." In *American Literature, 1764–1789: The Revolutionary Years,* edited by Everett Emerson, 39–57. Madison: University of Wisconsin Press, 1977.

Hirst, Désirée. *Hidden Riches: Traditional Symbolism from the Renaissance to Blake.* London: Eyre & Spottiswood, 1964.

Holbach, Baron Paul Henri Thiry d'. *History and Character of St. Paul Examined.* London: R. Carlile, 1823.

Howard, Leon. "The Late Eighteenth Century: An Age of Contradictions." In *Transitions in American Literary History,* edited by Harry Hayden Clark, 51–89. Durham: University of North Carolina Press, 1953.

Howard, Philip. *The Scripture History of the Earth and Mankind.* London, 1797.

Howell, T. B., and T. J. Howell. *A Complete Collection of State Trials and Proceedings for High Treason and Other Crimes and Misdemeanors.* 34 vols. London: T. C. Hansard, 1816–28.

Hunt, Lynn. "Hercules and the Radical Image in the French Revolution." *Representations* 2 (1983): 95–117.

Jacob, Margaret. *The Cultural Meaning of the Scientific Revolution.* Philadelphia: Temple University Press, 1988.

Jacob, Margaret, and James Jacob, eds. *The Origins of Anglo-American Radicalism.* London: Allen & Unwin, 1984.

Jamieson, John. *An Alarm in Britain: or, an Inquiry into the Causes of the Rapid Progress of Infidelity, in the Present Age.* Perth: R. Morison, Jr., 1795.

Jaspers, Karl, and Rudolf Bultmann. *Myth and Christianity: An Inquiry into the Possibility of Religion without Myth.* New York: Noonday Press, 1958.

Johnson, Samuel. *The Rambler.* Vol. 5 in *The Works of Samuel Johnson.* Edited by W. J. Bate and Albrecht B. Strauss. New Haven: Yale University Press, 1969.

Jones, Jeremiah. *New and Full Method of Settling the Canonical Authority of the New Testament.* 3 vols. Oxford: Clarendon Press, 1798.

Jordan, Cynthia S. *Second Stories: The Politics of Language, Form, and Gender in Early American Fictions.* Chapel Hill: University of North Carolina Press, 1989.

Jordan, Winthrop D. "Familial Politics: Thomas Paine and the Killing of the King, 1776." *Journal of American History* 60 (1973): 294–308.

Kates, Gary. "From Liberalism to Radicalism: Tom Paine's *Rights of Man.*" *Journal of the History of Ideas* 50 (1989): 569–87.

Kennedy, Michael L. *The Jacobin Clubs in the French Revolution: The First Years.* Princeton: Princeton University Press, 1982.

King, John Owen III. *The Iron of Melancholy: Structures of Spiritual Conversion in America from the Puritan Conscience to Victorian Neurosis.* Middletown, Conn.: Wesleyan University Press, 1983.

Koch, Adrienne, and William Peden, eds. *The Life and Seleced Letters of Thomas Jefferson.* New York: Modern Library, 1944.

Koester, Helmut. *History and Literature of Early Christianity.* Berlin: De Gruyth, 1982.

Kors, Alan Charles. *Atheism in France, 1650–1729.* Princeton: Princeton University Press, 1990.

———. *D'Holbach's Coterie: An Enlightenment in Paris.* Princeton: Princeton University Press, 1976.

Kouwenhoven, John A. *Made in America: The Arts in Modern American Civilization.* New York: W. W. Norton, 1967.

Kramnick, Isaac. *Republicanism and Bourgeois Radicalism: Political Ideology in Late-Eighteenth-Century England and America.* Ithaca: Cornell University Press, 1973.

Langford, Paul. *The First Rockingham Administration, 1765–1766.* Oxford: Oxford University Press, 1973.

Lardner, Nathaniel. *Credibility of the Gospel History.* London: John Gray, 1730.

Le Blond, Mrs. Aubrey. *Charlotte Sophie, Countess Bemtinck.* 2 vols. London: Hutchinson, 1912.

Levi, David. *Defence of the Old Testament, in a Series of Letters Addressed to Thomas Paine.* New York: William A. Davis, 1797.

Levine, Robert S. *Conspiracy and Romance: Studies in Brockden Brown, Cooper, Hawthorne, and Melville.* Cambridge: Cambridge University Press, 1989.

Levy, Leonard W. *Emergence of a Free Press.* New York: Oxford University Press, 1985.

Maccoby, S. *English Radicalism, 1786–1832: From Paine to Cobbett.* London: Allen & Unwin, 1955.

McGann, Jerome. "The Idea of an Indeterminate Text: Blake's Bible of Hell and Dr. Alexander Geddes." *Studies in Romanticism* 25 (1986): 303–24.

Macknight, James. *Harmony of the Gospels.* London: privately printed, 1756.

Manuel, Frank E. *The Eighteenth Century Confronts the Gods.* Cambridge: Harvard University Press, 1959.

Martin, Terence. "The Negative Structures of American Literature." *American Literature* 57 (1985): 1–22.

Middleton, Conyers. *A Free Inquiry into the Miraculous Powers Which Are Supposed to Have Subsisted in the Christian Church, from the Earliest Ages through Several Successive Centuries.* London: R. Manby and H. S. Cox, 1749.

———. *The Miscellaneous Works.* 4 vols. London: R. Manby and H. S. Cox, 1752.

Morgan, Robert, and John Barton. *Biblical Interpretation.* Oxford: Oxford University Press, 1988.

Neely, Sylvia. *Lafayette and the Liberal Ideal, 1814–1824: Politics and Conspiracy in an Age of Reaction.* Carbondale and Edwardsville: Southern Illinois University Press, 1991.

Newcome, William. *An Harmony of the Gospels.* Dublin, 1778.

Nord, David Paul. "A Republican Literature: Magazine Reading and Readers in Late-Eighteenth-Century New York." In *Reading in America: Literature and Social History,* edited by Cathy N. Davidson, 114–39. Baltimore: Johns Hopkins University Press, 1989.

O'Gorman, F. *The Whig Party and the French Revolution.* New York: St. Martin's Press, 1967.

Oldys, Francis. *The Life of Thomas Pain, the Author of the Seditious Writings Entitled the Rights of Man.* London: J. Stockdale, 1793.

Pagels, Elaine. *Adam, Eve, and the Serpent.* New York: Random House, 1988.

———. "The Politics of Paradise: Augustine's Exegesis of Genesis 1–3 Versus that of John Chrysostom." *Harvard Theological Review* 78 (1985): 67–95.

Paine, Thomas. *The Complete Writings of Thomas Paine.* 2 vols. Edited by Philip S. Foner. New York: Citadel Press, 1945.

Paley, William. *A View of the Evidence of Christianity.* 2 vols. London: R. Faulder, 1794.

Palmer, R. R. *The Age of the Democratic Revolution.* 2 vols. Princeton: Princeton University Press, 1959–64.

Patterson, Mark R. *Authority, Autonomy, and Representation in American Literature, 1776–1865.* Princeton: Princeton University Press, 1988.

Paulson, Ronald. "Burke's Sublime and the Representation of Revolution." In *Culture and Politics: From Puritanism to the Enlightenment,* edited by Perez Zagorin, 244–46. Berkeley: University of California Press, 1980.

Payne, Ernest A. "Tom Paine: Preacher." *Times Literary Supplement*, no. 2365 (31 May 1947): 267.

Payne, Michael. "Priestley, Paine, Blake, and the Tradition of English Dissent." *Pennsylvania English* 10 (1983): 5–13.

Pendleton, Gayle Trusde. "The English Pamphlet Literature of the Age of the French Revolution *Anatomized.*" *Eighteenth-Century Life* 5 (1978): 29–37.

———. "Towards a Bibliography of the *Reflections* and *Rights of Man* Controversy." *Bulletin of Research in the Humanities* 85 (1982): 65–103.

Popkin, Richard H. "The *Age of Reason* versus *The Age of Revelation:* Two Critics of Tom Paine." In *Deism, Masonry, and The Enlightenment,* edited by J. A. Leo Lemay, 158–70. Newark: University of Delaware Press, 1987.

———. *The History of Scepticism from Erasmus to Descartes*. New York: Harper Torchbooks, 1968.

Preston, Thomas P. "Biblical Criticism, Literature, and the Eighteenth-Century Reader." In *Books and Their Readers in Eighteenth-Century England.*, edited by Isabel Rivers, 97–126. New York: St. Martin's Press, 1982.

Price, Richard. *A Discourse on the Love of Our Country*. London: George Stafford, 1789.

Price, S. R. F. *Rituals and Power: The Roman Imperial Cult in Asia Minor*. Cambridge: Cambridge University Press, 1984.

Priestley, Joseph. *A Harmony of the Evangelists*. London: J. Johnson, 1795.

———. *Letters to a Philosophical Unbeliever*. Philadelphia: Thomas Dobson, 1795.

Reid, Chris. "Language and Practice in Burke's Political Writing." *Literature and History* 6 (1977): 203–18.

Ricoeur, Paul. *The Conflict of Interpretations: Essays in Hermeneutics*. Evanston, Ill.: Northwestern University Press, 1974.

Roe, Nicholas. *Wordsworth and Coleridge: The Radical Years*. Oxford: Clarendon Press, 1988.

Rogal, Samuel J. "Religious Periodicals in England during the Restoration and Eighteenth Century." *Journal of the Rutgers University Library* 35 (1971): 27–33.

Roth, Martin. "Tom Paine and American Loneliness." *Early American Literature* 22 (1988): 175–82.

Rothenberg, Molly Anne. "Parasiting America: The Radical Function of Heterogeneity in Thomas Paine's Early Writings." *Eighteenth-Century Studies* 25 (1992): 331–51.

Royle, Edward. *Radical Politics, 1790–1900: Religion and Unbelief.* London: Longman, 1971.

Rupp, Gordon. *Religion in England, 1688–1791*. Oxford: Clarendon Press, 1986.

Scheick, William J. "Benjamin Franklin and Lord Bute: Legendary Eighteenth-Century Representations." *Library Chronicle* 20, no. 3 (1990): 64–73.

Seavey, Ormond. *Becoming Benjamin Franklin: The "Autobiography" and the Life.* University Park: Pennsylvania State University Press, 1988.

Sennet, Richard. *Authority*. New York: Knopf, 1980.

———. *The Fall of Public Man*. New York: Vintage, 1978.

Shea, Daniel B., Jr. *Spiritual Autobiography in Early America*. Princeton: Princeton University Press, 1968.

Sherwin, W. T. *Memoir of the Life of Thomas Paine*. London: R. Carlile, 1819.

Smith, Jeffrey A. *Printers and Press Freedom: The Ideology of Early American Journalism*. New York: Oxford University Press, 1988.

Sommerville, C. John. *The Discovery of Childhood in Puritan England*. Athens: University of Georgia Press, 1992.

Spinoza, Benedict de. *The Chief Works of Benedict de Spinoza.* 2 vols. Translated by R. H. M. Elwes. New York: Dover, 1951.

———. *A Treatise Partly Theological, and Partly Political: The First English Edition.* London: 1689.

Stanlis, Peter J. *Edmund Burke and the Natural Law.* Ann Arbor: University of Michigan Press, 1958.

Steel, Emily Ellsworth Ford. *Mason Locke Weems: His Works and Ways in Three Volumes. A Bibliography Left Unfinished by Paul Leicester Ford.* 3 vols. New York: privately printed, 1929.

Sullivan, Alvin, ed. *British Literary Magazines: The Augustan Age and the Age of Johnson, 1698–1788.* Westport, Conn.: Greenwood Press, 1983.

Taylor, Thomas. *A Vindication of the Rights of Brutes.* Boston, Mass.: B. Sweetser and W. Burdick, 1795.

Tellenbach, Gerd. *Church, State, and Christian Society at the Time of the Investiture Contest.* Translated by R. F. Bennett. New York: Harper & Row, 1970.

Thompson, E. P. *The Making of the English Working Class.* New York: Pantheon, 1964.

Todd, William B. *A Bibliography of Edmund Burke.* London: Rupert Hart-Davis, 1964.

Toland, John. *Christianity not Mysterious; or a Treatise Shewing that there is nothing in the Gospel Contrary to Reason.* London, 1696.

Tolles, Frederick B. *Quakers and the Atlantic Culture.* New York: Macmillan, 1960.

Tomalin, Claire. *The Life and Death of Mary Wollstonecraft.* New York: Harcourt Brace Jovanovich, 1974.

Townson, Thomas. *A Discourse on the Evangelical History.* Oxford, 1793.

Turner, John. "Burke, Paine, and the Language of Assignats." *The Yearbook of English Studies* 19 (1989): 36–70.

Twomey, Richard J. *Jacobins and Jeffersonians: Anglo-American Radicalism in the United States, 1790–1820.* New York: Garland, 1989.

Wakefield, Gilbert. *An Examination of "The Age of Reason."* Worcester, Mass.: Isaiah Thomas, 1794.

Walker, Robert. *Analysis of Researches into the Origin and Progress of Historical Time.* London, 1796.

Ward, William S. *Literary Reviews in British Periodicals, 1789–1797: A Bibliography.* New York: Garland, 1979.

Warner, Michael. *The Letters of the Republic: Publication and the Public Sphere in Eighteenth-Century America.* Cambridge: Harvard University Press, 1990.

Watson, Richard. *The Apology for the Bible.* New York: T. & J. Swords, 1796.

Weber, Donald. *Rhetoric and History in Revolutionary New England.* New York: Oxford University Press, 1988.

Whately, Richard. *Essays on Some of the Dangers to Christian Faith.* London: B. Fellows, 1839.

Wilkins, Burleigh Taylor. *The Problem of Burke's Political Philosophy.* Oxford: Clarendon Press, 1967.

Williamson, Audrey. *Thomas Paine: His Life, Work, and Times.* London: George Allen & Unwin, 1973.

Wilson, Jerome D. "Thomas Paine in America: An Annotated Bibliography, 1900–1973." *Bulletin of Bibliography* 31 (1974): 133–56.

Wilson, Jerome D., and William E. Ricketson. *Thomas Paine: Updated Edition.* Boston: Twayne, 1989.

Wollstonecraft, Mary. *An Historical and Moral View of the Origin and Progress of the French Revolution; and the Effect It Has Produced in Europe.* London: J. Johnson, 1794.

Index

DATE DUE

			Printed in USA